SACRAMENTO KINGS

An *Interactive* Guide to the World of Sports

SB

Savas Beatie

New York and California

Printed in the United States of America

This book is not sponsored, officially endorsed by, or affiliated with, the subject team.

Cataloging-in-Publication Data is available from the Library of Congress.

ISBN 13: 978-1-932714-69-2

10 09 08 07 06 05 04 03 02 01
First edition, first printing

SB
Published by
Savas Beatie LLC
521 Fifth Avenue, Suite 1700
New York, NY 10175
Phone: 610-853-9131

Editorial Offices:

Savas Beatie LLC
P.O. Box 4527
El Dorado Hills, CA 95762
Phone: 916-941-6896
(E-mail) editorial@savasbeatie.com

Also by Daniel J. Brush, David Horne, and Marc CB Maxwell

NASCAR
University of Oklahoma Football
New York Yankees
Major League Baseball
Mixed Martial Arts (with Zac Robinson)
University of Georgia Football (with Keith Gaddie)
San Francisco Giants (with Zac Robinson)

Also by Marc CB Maxwell

Surviving Military Separation: 365 Days
An Activity Guide for Family Members of Deployed Personnel
Illustrated by Val Laolagi
(Savas Beatie, 2007)

For

Gary Grace

The “King” of Coaching

Contents

Contents (continued)

Contents (continued)

Photos, illustrations, charts, and tables have been placed throughout the book for the benefit of our readers.

Foreword

This book on the Sacramento Kings is part of the intriguing and exciting *Sports by the Numbers*™ series, which is published by Savas Beatie LLC, a local publishing company with strong ties to our community. When its Managing Director, Theodore "Ted" Savas, asked me to write this Foreword, I happily agreed to do so for a number of reasons. First, to share with others information about the Boys & Girls Clubs of Greater Sacramento. Second, to thank Bank of America for its long support of our program and for making this book possible. And last but certainly not least, because I love basketball in general, and the Sacramento Kings in particular!

The Boys & Girls Clubs of Greater Sacramento (BGCGS) was founded in 1996 in response to a growing need in our community for constructive after-school programs for youth. Our mission is to inspire and enable all young people, especially those who need us most, to realize their full potential as productive, responsible, and caring citizens. We offer programs at two full service club facilities: the Raley Branch in downtown Sacramento, and the Teichert Branch in Lemon Hill. In 2007, we also began providing school-based after-school programs at seven area elementary schools.

As the BGCGS' Chief Executive Officer, I am often asked what, exactly, kids do in our programs. In a nutshell, we provide safe havens for young people where they can:

- Play games and have fun;

- Do homework and get academic assistance;
- Develop positive health and nutrition habits;
- Learn life skills, such as responsible decision-making, problem-solving, and goal-setting;
- Learn transferable skills related to technology, work, careers, and higher education

Every Boys & Girls Club program across America incorporates the Youth Development Strategy, which fosters a sense of belonging, competence, usefulness, and influence among young people. These programs help participants develop self-confidence and self-esteem that they can carry with them for a lifetime. My job is always rewarding, but it is never easy.

BGCGS serves youth ages 6 – 18. We have more than 2,700 registered members, with daily attendance ranging from 300 – 600. The majority of our member population lives in South Sacramento, in neighborhoods with large youth populations, including Lemon Hill, Fruitridge, and Meadowview. The remainder live in the downtown Sacramento neighborhood of Alkali Flat. Our membership is culturally diverse, with a mixture of long-term residents and recent immigrants and newcomers. Seventy percent of our members come from economically challenged backgrounds (family income $23,000 or less) and 42% live in single parent families. Membership is just $12 per school year, but it costs our Club $562 a year to provide programs. (Keep in mind it costs the state of California more than $25,000 to house one inmate for one year!)

This short introduction about our club leads me to my next reason for writing this Foreword. Many individuals and organizations help support BGCGS. Without their help, we would not be able to serve our youth. Bank of America has steadfastly assisted us over the years. In addition to financial support, this year the bank agreed to help us implement a fun, educational, and exciting way to promote reading, writing, math, web technologies, and more. How? By helping sponsor the book you are now holding in your hands.

Eric Stanion, Bank of America's Senior Vice President, Market Development Manager, spearheaded this project. Eric worked closely with the publisher, Marketing Director Sarah Keeney, and myself to make sure the book was suitable for our program, and that it would help facilitate literacy within our group. Savas Beatie agreed to prepare what is now known as Sports by the Numbers in a Box™, a series of games, lesson plans, ideas, and programs based around the *Sacramento Kings* book that our staff and students can easily implement. This book is filled with short and fun-to-read stories about our Sacramento Kings, each tied to a number, and in turn related to a dynamic website. We are confident our youth members will not only love reading all of them, but will learn from them and participate in the cool projects we have planned around this amazing book!

Finally, this book is all about basketball, and our youth love the NBA in general, and the Sacramento Kings in particular! The Kings bring so much to our community: pride in a professional team, community service, great games, an outstanding cast of personalities, and owners in the Maloofs who have always supported important programs that help greater Sacramento. The concept of these books is wonderful, but the subject matter of this book really excites our young people. Because of that excitement, they will read more, think more, participate more, and root *longer* and **louder** for their Sacramento Kings!

Thank you Eric, Ted, Sarah, and everyone else for your steadfast support of Boys & Girls Club of Greater Sacramento.

And go Kings!

Kim Williams
Chief Executive Officer
Boys & Girls Club of Greater Sacramento

Preface

Numbers are a language that everyone understands. We can tell who won, who scored more, and what players are on track for the Hall of Fame by looking at their numbers. We use the box scores to see if our Sacramento Kings are going to the playoffs and if your team isn't. Fans use these numbers to validate their team's losing season and to compare today's heroes to those of yesteryear. Numbers and statistics allow us to compare Kevin Martin to Oscar Robertson, Mike Bibby to Jack Twyman, and Peja Stojakovic to Nate Archibald.

Numbers tell the stories that make "our" team great. They show how our Royals won an NBA title and the reason why others got away (see 2002 Western Conference Finals vs. LA). Numbers of players are immortalized at ARCO Arena. Kids wear the numbers of their favorite players like Bobby Jackson while we (sometimes) scoff at the numbers in a specific player's paycheck. We obsess over stats because they all tell a story.

It was on this premise that we created the Sports by the Numbers franchise in July of 2006. It began in Rudy's "Country Store" and Bar-B-Q, one of our favorite hangout spots in Norman, Oklahoma. On the big screen TV the Atlanta Braves and the St. Louis Cardinals were in the midst of a lopsided affair for the second consecutive day. It was the Braves offense posting the big numbers, 29 runs in two games. Atlanta, of course, was hoping to make a post-season push after winning 14 consecutive division titles since 1991. We did the math on a napkin, and we decided the odds were long against the Braves making it 15 straight. Statistically, it was a mind-numbing streak, and as our conversation drifted among sports, numbers, and memories, we began talking about streaks, and about records that will never be broken.

Some of the people around us were listening to our conversation, though we did not realize it until we stood to leave at the same time as an older gentleman who was seated at a table behind us. He gave us a nod and said, "Forty-seven." Then he smiled, "The longest winning streak in NCAA history, set by OU."

His interest in our conversation validated what we knew to be true already—that sports fans are passionate about numbers and the stories they tell. It took us only a few days to draft a proposal for the Sports by the Numbers series, and only a few days more to draft some samples for the University of Oklahoma title. It took only a few weeks to find the right publisher, who then got the perfect website designer for us, and began helping us to craft the format of the books to tell our stories in the best way possible.

In every SBTN title, you will find a numerical list from one to one thousand—and for each number the SBTN team will give you a story by way of statistical facts, anomalies, records, personalities, accomplishments, and fascinating trivia. If you love sports, our books are for you. If you have a hero from your favorite team, our books are for you. If you want to learn about a sport or a specific team, our books are for you.

Our books, however, are not just for diehards like us. If you want to teach a new fan about a team or sport, then SBTN is perfect for that too. But just in case you are as passionate and obsessive of a fan as we are, look for future SBTN titles on your favorite sports and your favorite teams, and reminisce with us about days gone by and championships won and lost.

The SBTN experience does not end with the books. Inside each title you will find that our favorite numbers are tagged as SBTN – All Star or SBTN – Hall of Fame. When you see those, go online to www.sportsbythenumbers.com and use those specific numbers to access more content on the web and take part in our SBTN Interactive World of Sports. You will also find on our website some of our SBTN memories. We invite you to check them out, and email us some of your own so we can post them on our site too.

We hope you enjoy this Sacramento Kings version of Sports by the Numbers™ as much as we enjoyed putting it together for you . . . the fan!

Acknowledgments

It is time to acknowledge so many important people who have made this SBTN book a reality.

First and foremost, to Dr. James Naismith for creating one of the greatest games ever. Fans and players owe so much to you for giving us this gift.

To Kings and Royals players past and present: Thank you for giving us a show each and every time you grace that hardwood court.

Special thanks to Theodore P. "Ted" Savas of Savas Beatie Publishing. Thank you for believing in our vision and making this book possible.

To Sarah Keeney, Marketing Director for Savas Beatie: Your work on this title was invaluable. We appreciate all your support on each and every SBTN manuscript.

Our website and logo designer is Val Laolagi, and he was introduced to us by our publisher as the best talent on the market for this sort of work. His vision for the website is amazing, and we are grateful to be surrounded by such talent.

Jim Zach of zGrafix designs many of the books produced by Savas Beatie. He also creates the best book covers on the sports market today—and he does it for SBTN.

To Eric Stanion of the Bank of America, Sacramento, for realizing how SBTN titles can be used to help educate and enlighten young and old alike.

To our parents: Bill and Dorthe Brush, Larry and Connie Horne, and Richard and Deanna Maxwell. For every basket you shot with us, for every one-on-one game we played in the backyard, for every contest of H-O-R-S-E, we are eternally grateful.

Finally, all three of us were blessed and found someone to make us better people—Paulina Brush, Lisa Horne, and Christine Maxwell. Thank you for believing in us.

Daniel J. Brush, David Horne,
and Marc CB Maxwell
Norman, Oklahoma
October 8, 2008

The Locker

Welcome to Sports by the Numbers™ and our Interactive Guide to the World of Sports. In compiling our first 1,000 numbers that we used to tell stories in our debut title, *University of Oklahoma Football*, it was apparent to us that for one reason or another some of the numbers resonated more deeply with us than did others—they were special.

The numbers were all great, but there were some numbers that we were drawn towards and felt the need to expand on more than the others. Our website provided us with the opportunity to do just that in an area we call The Locker.

The team of authors for this title on the Sacramento Kings has used special logos to designate five Hall of Fame numbers and ten All-Star numbers that you will come across as you read the stories that unfold within these pages.

Numbers designated as Hall of Fame or All-Star lets you know that they are among our favorites from this book—and once in the locker room, you will find out why.

Our website is: www.SportsByTheNumbers.com

Use the tab at the top of our homepage or the locker on the bottom right-hand corner of our homepage to enter our locker. Once there you will see the covers of all the SBTN titles that are currently available.

Click on the cover of your favorite SBTN title to view the Hall of Fame and All-Star numbers that the SBTN authors have selected for that book.

You can then click on any number in the locker room to gain access to additional information that may come in the form of pictures, video, audio, text, or random musings from one of the SBTN authors, but regardless, it will enhance the story told by the number, and it will let you know why we feel the number is so significant.

Creating an Interactive World of Sports that combines the best of the traditional book world with the unlimited potential of the Internet is an exciting and fluid process—and we are constantly working on new and better ways to bring together the book world and the cyber world with one goal in mind, to give sports fans the ultimate experience when it comes to reminiscing about their favorite numbers, players, teams, and memories.

Enjoy the experience!

Rochester Royals 1950-51 World Championship Roster

Record: 41-27

Home Arena: Edgerton Park Arena

Scored 84.6 points per game, Allowed 81.7 points per game

Les Harrison, Head Coach
Bill Calhoun
Jack Coleman
Bob Davies
Red Holzman
Arnie Johnson
Joe McNamee
Paul Noel
Arnie Risen
Pep Saul
Bobby Wanzer

Playoffs:

- Won NBA Finals (4-3) versus New York Knicks
- Won NBA Western Division Finals (3-1) versus Minneapolis Lakers
- Won NBA Western Division Semifinals (2-1) versus Fort Wayne Pistons

"I think we did have a superior team and we were well aware of it."

— Arnie Risen, NBA Hall of Famer
and Rochester Royal World Champion

Chapter One

World Champions

Sacramento fans know it's coming. It's only a matter of time before they return to a World Championship series and hoist the Larry O'Brien Championship Trophy. Unfortunately for the Sacramento faithful, the Kings have endured the pain of having the longest NBA Championship and NBA Finals appearance drought.

But at least we have one!

There are so many clubs in the league that cannot claim a NBA title to their team's résumé. The Los Angeles Clippers, Denver Nuggets, Phoenix Suns, Cleveland Cavaliers, Utah Jazz, Indiana Pacers, New Jersey Nets, and the Dallas Mavericks to name a few.

It may have been a long time since the Kings' organization was on top, but tasting victory once means you've been there and done that. A perfect example of this logic is the Boston Red Sox and their amazing turnaround after battling the Curse of the Bambino for 86 years. The

Kings are nowhere near that kind of drought, and with a youthful line-up in Sacramento, the Kings are guaranteed to win another title.

It was 1951 and the Rochester Royals had just come off a disappointing finish the year before after rolling through the regular season at 51-17. Their 2-0 Central Division Semifinals loss to the Fort Wayne Pistons gave the Royals the added fuel they needed. With future Hall of Famers Arnie Risen, Bob Davies, and Bobby Wanzer leading the way, the only thing that separated them from a NBA title was the dynasty of George Mikan and the Minneapolis Lakers.

After trampling their opponents during the regular season and recording a 41-27 record, the Royals slid past the Pistons in the first round of the playoffs 2-1. Next came the Lakers and George Mikan. After losing the first game of the series 76-73 in Minneapolis, the Royals regrouped and handed an injured Mikan a 70-66 loss before moving the series to Rochester.

With Mikan nursing a leg injury, the Royals took it to them and finished with an 83-70 victory and an 80-75 win to close out the series 3-1. Next up was the New York Knicks, who had survived the Boston Celtics and the Syracuse Nationals earlier in the playoffs.

"It was like every year we were a bridesmaid but never the bride," Bobby Wanzer said. "And finally, we beat Minneapolis and then we went on and we faced New York. We always figured that the two best teams at that time in basketball were Minneapolis and the Royals. So once we were free of Minneapolis, we thought we had a cinch."

Guess again.

After winning the first three games of the series, the Royals looked like they were destined for a sweep. The Democrat and Chronicle's headline read, "That Was Neat! Now Let's Go For the Sweep!" Luckily for the NBA which was trying to build a fan base, the Knicks roared back making a boring series anything but. The Knicks captured the next three games forcing a winner-take-all Game 7. The game was played in Rochester and came down to the final seconds with Bob Davies knocking down two free throws with 44 seconds left on the clock. Another basket followed with three seconds on the clock as the Royals won the game 79-75, earning the franchise their only title to date.

Risen posted a 21.7 points per game average during the series, Davies averaged 17 points and 5.3 assists, and Wanzer scored 12.4 points per game to bring the title to Rochester. After the game, Head Coach Les

Harrison took the Royals out on the town and paid for their dinner. There were no parades for the team either. There were no championship rings at that time; only the satisfaction of winning it all.

Satisfaction that Kings' fans long for, but know is coming. . .

1 The number of World Championships (1) hoisted by the Kings organization. During the 1950-51 season, the precursor Rochester Royals finished the regular season with a 41-27 record. The squad went on to beat the New York Knicks, 4 games to 3 in the NBA Finals, while team leader Arnie Risen scored 19.5 points per game during the playoffs.

2 Number of times (2) Oscar Robertson scored 43 points in a playoff game. Robertson hit the mark against the Boston Celtics twice in the same year, 1963. The 43 points marks the most points scored in a single playoff game by a Kings player.

3 The number of players (3) who have worn the jersey number 00. Tony Delk, Art Long, and Greg Ostertag have all worn the double naught jersey. Olden Polynice is the only player in team history to have worn the number zero.

4 Most three-point field goals (4) made by a Kings player during a playoff game. This feat was achieved by Jason Williams during the April 23, 2000 game versus the LA Lakers.

5 The number of cities (5) that have adopted the Kings organization. The team originally started as the Rochester Royals and then moved on to become the Cincinnati Royals. After, the squad was claimed by Kansas City and Omaha as the Kings and a few years later that became just the Kansas City Kings. Finally, in 1985, the team was introduced as the Sacramento Kings.

6 The number of steals (6) recorded by Ernie Grunfeld versus the Houston Rockets during their April 26, 1981 playoff game. Two days

earlier, Sam Lacey also recorded six take-a-ways against the Rockets. These six swipes ties the Kings record for most steals in a playoff game, originally set by Bill Robinzine vs. Phoenix on April 20, 1979.

7 Most blocked shots (7) by a Kings player during a playoff game, set by Chris Webber vs. the Los Angeles Lakers during their May 2, 2000 meeting.

8 Unfortunately, the number of most turnovers (8) recorded by a Kings player during the playoffs. This notorious record was set by Sam Lacey during the April 25, 1979 matchup versus the Phoenix Suns.

9 Number of offensive rebounds (9) recorded by Darnell Hillman at Phoenix during the teams' April 27, 1979 playoff meeting. This is a Kings record for most offensive rebounds snagged during a post-season game.

10 Jersey number (10) for Nathaniel "Tiny" Archibald from 1971-74. The 1991 Hall of Fame inductee also donned the jersey number 1 when playing for the Kansas City – Omaha Kings in 1975 and with the KC Kings in 1976.

11 Jersey number (11) of Hall of Fame inductee Bob Davies during his stay with the Rochester Royals from 1949-55. The four time All-Star was also a four time 1st team All-NBA selection while scoring 6,594 points with the Kings organization.

12 Jersey number (12) of Hall of Fame inductee Maurice Stokes. In 1956 he was selected as the NBA Rookie of the Year. A member of the Rochester and Cincinnati Royals, Stokes' career was cut short. On the last regular season game of his third year, Stokes fell to the floor and hit his head. He fell into a coma and was permanently paralyzed, but continued to inspire others for the remainder of his life.

13 Overall selection (13) during the 1995 NBA draft for the Kings Corliss "Big Nasty" Williamson. Williamson was Big *and* Nasty even as a twelve year old. During the 1986 AAU National Basketball

Championships for 12-and-unders in Bellevue, Washington the Big Nasty was 6'1" and towered over his opponents.

14 Jersey number (14) of Hall of Fame inductee Oscar Robertson. Before playing for the Kings organization, "The Big O" played his college ball at Cincinnati where he led the Bearcats to an overall record of 79-9, including two Final Four appearances. The College Player of the Year Award was renamed the Oscar Robertson Trophy in 1998. Robertson won the first two of these awards in 1959 and 1960.

15 Number of loses (15) recorded by the Rochester Royals during their first season. The team completed the season with an overall record of 45-15 and a .750 winning percentage. The team finished first during the Western Division regular season before falling in the playoffs to the Minneapolis Lakers.

16 Number of playoff games (16) the Kings participated in during the 2002 post-season. After disposing of the Utah Jazz in the first-round, the Kings beat up on the Dallas Mavericks 4-1 in the Western Conference Semifinals. The team eventually lost to the Los Angeles Lakers 4 games to 3 in the Conference Finals. The series was plagued with questionable calls by some referees and has left many experts to wonder if the series was rigged; negating what may have been Sacramento's best chance at an NBA title in years.

17 Number of charter member teams (17) that made up the original NBA league. The Sacramento franchise was one of the founding 17 clubs when a merger between the Basketball Association of America and the National Basketball League was formed.

18 Number of locker stalls (18) for players in the Kings Practice Facility which is adjacent to ARCO Arena. The $9.1 million facility opened its doors in December of 2000. Besides the 18 stalls, the locker rooms also have a 63-inch high definition plasma television with DVD player, 10-speaker stereo system, and individual monogrammed robes and towels for the players.

19 Lowest number of wins (19) recorded by a Kings team during the 1960 and 1961 seasons. Both Cincinnati Royals squads finished the regular season with less than a .265 winning percentage. Needless to say, neither team made the playoffs.

20 Number of years (20) documented in the book *Reynolds Remembers: 20 Years with the Sacramento Kings* by Jerry Reynolds. Reynolds has served as the Kings head coach, scout, general manager, and television analyst. The book was released in 2005.

21 Jersey number (21) of Serbian born hooper Vlade Divac during his six seasons with the Sacramento Kings from 1999-2004. For his work with the community, Divac was awarded the J. Walter Kennedy Citizenship Award for the 1999-2000 season.

22 Team leading number of steals per game average (2.2) during a career by the Kings' Ron Artest through the 2008 season. Artest has led the NBA in steal percentage twice. In 2002, Artest recorded a 4.5 steal percentage and in 2003, he tallied a 3.6 percentage.

23 Number of wins (23) collected by the 1989-90 Sacramento Kings. This was the lowest win output by a King' team in the 1980s or the 1990s. Not surprisingly, the team didn't make the playoffs that season. It would take six more seasons for Sacramento to see the postseason after making the playoffs in 1985-86.

24 Number of points (24) scored in Game 7 of the 1951 NBA Championships by the Rochester Royals' Arnie Risen. The four time NBA All-Star scored 1,077 points that year during the regular season, but none were as important as the 24 he pumped in during the deciding game which resulted in a Royals victory.

25 Franchise record for most three-point field goal attempts (25) jacked up by a Kings team during a playoff game. The Kings trey'd it up a record amount of times vs. the Dallas Mavericks on May 17, 2003.

26 The number of minutes (26) played by Cincinnati Royals' guard Adrian Smith during his sole NBA All-Star appearance in 1966.

Smith took home All-Star MVP honors that year after chipping in 24 points for the East squad as they annihilated the West, 137-94.

27 Retired jersey number (27) of Jack Twyman. The former University of Cincinnati star was the sixth player in NBA history to score 15,000 points. Side note: Twyman also wore numbers 10 and 31 for the Kings organization.

28 Kings' franchise record for most rebounds (28) secured by a King/Royal during a playoff game, set by Jack Coleman vs. New York on April 8, 1951.

29 The number of playoff appearances (29) recorded by the Sacramento Kings, the Kansas City Kings, the Kansas City – Omaha Kings, the Cincinnati Royals, and the Rochester Royals. The first seven years in the league, the Rochester Royals made the playoffs each season, winning it all in just their third season. After failing to reach the playoffs in two consecutive seasons, the team moved to Cincinnati and made the playoffs their first season there despite posting a losing record. They would make the playoffs six more times during their 15 seasons in Cincinnati before moving to Kansas City. As either the KC-Omaha or Kansas City Kings, the team would make the playoffs five times in 13 years before ending up in Sacramento. Since 1985, the Kings have made the playoffs ten times.

30 Number of luxury seats (30) at ARCO Arena, home of the Sacramento Kings. The 40 million dollar stadium opened its doors in 1988 and is located at One Sports Parkway in Sacramento, California.

31 Draft selection (31) for the Kings Assistant Coach Randy Brown during the 1991 NBA draft. Brown spent 12 seasons in the league and earned three World Championship rings with Chicago in 1996, 1997, and 1998.

32 Franchise record for most field goal attempts (32) put up by a King in a postseason game. This record was set by Chris Webber vs. Phoenix on April 22, 2001.

33 Number of wins (33) posted by Head Coach Eddie Jordan during his tenure with the Kings. Jordan tallied a .340 winning percentage before being relieved of his duties on August 18, 1998.

34 Number of field goal attempts (34) tossed up by Houston's Moses Malone on April 26, 1981. This is a record for most shot attempts vs. the Kings by an opponent during a playoff contest.

35 Franchise record for most assists (35) dished out by a Kings/Royals team during a playoff game. The record was compiled at Portland vs. the Trailblazers on April 1, 1981.

36 Number of games (36) played by Andrew Levane during his 1949 season with the Rochester royals. Levane, a former St. John's University standout, later became head coach of the Milwaukee Hawks, New York Knicks, and the St. Louis Hawks.

37 Kings franchise record for most assists (37) dished out by a Kings/Royals' opponent during a postseason game. The Phoenix Suns dealt out 37 lend-a-hands on April 6, 1980.

38 Number of loses (38) tallied by the Sacramento Kings during the 2006 season. The Kings finished the season with a winning record by posting 44 wins. Mike Bibby led the team with 444 assists and a 21.1 ppg average.

39 Sacramento Kings era record for most points (39) scored in a single postseason game. The record was set by Peja Stojakovic on May 10, 2003 vs. the Dallas Mavericks in a double overtime thriller.

40 Through the 2008 NBA campaign, the number of times (40) the Kings and Miami Heat have played one another. The Heat holds the series lead at 24-16, but averages less than two more points per contest, 98-96.3.

41 Total number of wins (41) secured by the Rochester Royals during their 1951 NBA championship season. The Royals finished the year at 41-27.

42 Overall pick selection (42) by the Kings for Sean Singletary of the University of Virginia during the 2008 NBA draft. During his last season at UVA, the senior broke the 2,000 point mark, making him one of only three players in ACC history to score 2,000 points, hand out 500 assists, and grab 400 rebounds. The other two players are Duke legends Danny Ferry and Johnny Dawkins.

43 An unfortunate record: Number of consecutive games (43) that the Los Angeles Lakers triumphed over the Sacramento Kings. The streak spanned over 18 years with the Kings winning on October 20, 1974 and not again until November 8, 1992.

44 Team leading career number of minutes played per game (44) by a Kings franchise player, recorded by Hall of Famer Oscar Robertson. The nine time 1st team All-NBA selection recorded 43,886 minutes played during his career.

45 Retired Portland Trailblazers jersey number (45) of Sacramento Kings' General Manager Geoff Petrie. The two-time NBA All-Star played his college ball at Princeton.

46 NBA league leading number of points per game average (46), collected by the Kings' Nathaniel Archibald during the 1973 season. This would be the only time he would lead this category during his career. Amazingly, he also led the league in assists per game that same year with 11.4 lend-a-hands per game.

47 Number of free throws (47) made by Rochester Royal Thomas Marshall during his 1957 NBA campaign. That season, Marshall chipped in 159 points during his 40 games played.

48 The number of victories (48) posted by the 1978-79 Kansas City Kings. Under first year coach Cotton Fitzsimmons, the Kings would post a 48-34 record on the season and win the Midwest Division title. Despite getting knocked out 4-1 in the Western Conference Semifinals by the Phoenix Suns, the first year coach won Coach of the Year honors after taking a team 20 games below .500 one season earlier and turning them into division champs.

49 Number of games (49) played by Larry Staverman during his 1960 season with the Cincinnati Royals. The 6'7" forward from Thomas More College spent five years in the NBA. He would later serve as the first head coach of the Indiana Pacers.

50 Number of games (50) played by Steve Johnson during his 1984 season with the Kansas City Kings. The former Oregon State standout played under the legendary coach Ralph Miller before turning pro. While in the NBA, Johnson would play for the Kings, Bulls, Spurs, Trailblazers, Timberwolves, Sonics, and Warriors.

51 Team record for most points (51) scored by a Sacramento King in an overtime game. This record was set by Chris Webber vs. Indiana on January 5, 2001.

52 Year ('52) that the Rochester Royals won a Western Division crown. Paul Noel, a reserve who saw limited action during the year, shot .667 from the charity stripe while logging in 32 minutes of court time in eight games. Although he hardly broke a sweat during game days, one thing he can claim is that he was part of a championship team!

53 Basketball Association of America league leading number of assists per game (5.3) for 1970 Hall of Fame inductee Bob Davies during his 1948-49 season with the Royals. This would be the only time in Davies' career that he would lead the league in this category even though he dished out six lend-a-hands per game in 1952.

54 Kings franchise record for most free throws (54) shot during a postseason contest. The record was earned at Boston on March 27, 1966.

55 Team record for fewest points (55) scored by a Kings/Royals squad during a playoff game. The record was set vs. the Minneapolis Lakers game on March 29, 1949.

56 ARCO Arena record for most turnovers (56) recorded by two teams, set on March 7, 1995 when the Kings played the Utah Jazz. During the game, the Kings committed 31 turnovers to Utah's 25.

57 Team record for most free throws (57) attempted by a Sacramento squad, set by the Kings vs. Utah on April 20, 1997.

58 Number of career playoff wins (58) during 18 NBA seasons by William "Red" Holzman. Holzman was inducted into the HOF in 1986 and is one of only a handful of people to win a championship as a player and a coach. As a player, Red reached the pinnacle with the 1951 Rochester Royals as they beat the NY Knicks in seven games. Years later he led those same Knicks to the 1970 and 1973 NBA World title as head coach.

59 Kings/Royals record for most points (59) scored in a single contest, set by Jack Twyman vs. Minneapolis on January 15, 1960.

60 ARCO Arena record for most field goals (60) made in a half of play by two teams, set by the Kings and Golden State. Sacramento tossed in 25 hoops while the Warriors popped in 35 shots on January 21, 1989.

61 Franchise record for number of wins (61) during a regular season. The 2001-02 team recorded a .744 winning percentage after posting a 61-21 record. To date, this is the only time in franchise history that the Kings have won more than 60 games.

62 ARCO Arena record for most field goals (62) attempted in a half of play by one team, set by the Portland Trailblazers vs. the Kings on April 18, 1989.

63 Sacramento Kings team record for most field goals (63) attempted in a half of play, set on April 2, 1987 vs. the Los Angeles Clippers.

64 The 2008-09 season is the Kings' (64th) season as a franchise including a three year stint in the National Basketball League. This is the Kings' 61st season in the NBA.

65 Ultimate Fighting Championship (65) *Bad Intentions* was conducted at ARCO Arena on November 18, 2006 and highlighted two

World Championship title fights (Hughes vs. St. Pierre and Sylvia vs. Monson).

66 NBA league leading number of games (66) played by 1987 Hall of Fame inductee Bobby Wanzer during his 1951-52 season with the Rochester Royals. That same season, Wanzer also topped the NBA charts with a .904 free throw percentage.

67 Kings/Royals team record for most field goals (67) made during a single game, set on March 12, 1970 vs. San Diego.

68 Amount of dollars (68) in the millions that Brad Miller's contract was negotiated for moments before being traded to the Kings by the Indiana Pacers in a five-player trade that included the Kings, Pacers, and San Antonio Spurs. The five players involved in the trade were Miller, Scot Pollard, Hedo Turkoglu, Danny Ferry, and Ron Mercer.

69 Number of points (69) scored by Indianapolis during a 1951-52 overtime victory vs. the Rochester Royals. This is the only time in the history of the franchise that a Kings opponent scored 69 points in an overtime contest.

70 Year ('70) that Boston Celtics' legend Bob Cousy came on as the Cincinnati Royals head coach. That year Cousy ended the season with a 36-46 record and a .439 winning percentage.

71 Month and day (7/1) in 1999 that the Maloof family took control over the Kings organization and ARCO Arena, previously owned by Jim Thomas since April 6, 1992.

72 Number of games (72) played by Maurice Stokes during the 1956-57 season. That year, Stokes pulled down 1,256 rebounds for an NBA league leading average of 17.4 boards per game.

73 ARCO Arena record for most free throws (73) made by two teams in a regulation contest. The record was set by the Kings and the Miami Heat in a January 9, 1993 matchup. The Kings sank 37 free throws to Miami's 36.

74 Number of game broadcasts (74) that *Comcast SportsNet* transmitted as the Kings' Cable Flagship during the 2007-08 season. The network also managed the Kings' radio and television advertisement and sponsorship sales for those broadcasts.

75 Number of loses (75) compiled by the Kings franchise during overtime games played at home from 1945-2007. During that stretch, the franchise was able to win 59 home overtime games.

76 Year ('76) that two time NBA and three time ABA All-Star Larry Kenon set the NBA record for most steals (11) in a single game while playing for San Antonio. He recorded this feat on December 26, 1976 vs. the Kansas City Kings.

77 Points per game average (7.7) posted by Bill Calhoun during his 1951 campaign with the World Champion Rochester Royals. The former City College of San Francisco star wore jersey #19 for the Royals from 1949-51.

78 Number of field goal attempts (78) jacked up by the Sacramento Kings vs. the Houston Rockets on March 20, 2001. The Kings made 51 of those shots for a Sacramento era record for best shooting percentage in one contest by a Kings' club at .654.

79 Number of games (79) played by Oscar Robertson during the 1962 season. That year, Robertson dished out a NBA league leading 899 assists while averaging 11.4 a game.

80 Numbers of games (80) played by Nate Archibald during his 1973 NBA campaign. Although other players in the league played just as many games, no one played more minutes. Tiny ended the season with 3,681 minutes played.

81 Number of points (81) surrendered by the Kings in their November 6, 2006 home opener vs. the Minnesota Timberwolves. The Kings won the game 93-81 as Ron Artest tallied 22 points and eight rebounds for the Kings while Kevin Martin added 19 points for the cause.

82 Team leading number of games (82) played by Mikki Moore during the Kings' 2007-08 season. Moore is the only player on the squad who saw action in all 82 games. He started 79 of those contests while averaging 8.5 points per game.

83 Franchise record for most points (83) surrendered in a half of play by a Kings/Royals defense during a postseason game. The Dallas Mavericks shot lights out on May 8, 2003.

84 Last year ('84) that Cotton Fitzsimmons would coach the Kings organization. The Missouri Sports Hall of Fame inductee and two-time National Junior College champion with Moberly Junior College had two stints with the Kings, from 1978-79 and again from 1983-84.

85 Year ('85) that the Kings moved from Kansas City to Sacramento to set up their new home at ARCO Arena. Since the move, the Kings have won two division titles, in 2002 and 2003.

86 *Topps Bowman* basketball card number (86) of the Sacramento Kings' Quincy Douby for his 2007 autographed *Sterling Rookie Refractor* card. The series has 199 total cards dedicated to NBA hoopers.

87 ARCO Arena record for most points (87) scored by two teams in a quarter. This record was set during the fourth quarter by the Sacramento Kings (46) vs. the New Jersey Nets (41) on March 16, 1994.

88 Number of touchdowns (88) tossed by Pro Football Hall of Famer Otto Graham during his ten seasons of pro ball. He spent six seasons in the NFL, winning three World titles. He also won a National Basketball League title with the 1946 Rochester Royals before they moved into the NBA.

89 Overall selection (89) by the Kansas City Kings in the 1976 NBA draft for UCLA guard Andre McCarter. McCarter was selected in the sixth round and ended up playing 60 games for the Kings while compiling 270 points.

90 Year ('90) that the Sacramento Kings named Dick Motta, the third winningest coach in NBA history, head coach. Motta was relieved of his duties with the Kings in December of 1991. Before he came on board in Sacramento, he won an NBA Championship with the Washington Bullets. Many fans mistakenly believe Motta coined the phrase "It ain't over 'til the fat lady sings," during the 1978 NBA Finals series between his Bullets and the Seattle Supersonics. However, what he really said was, "The opera ain't over 'til the fat lady sings" . . . a rendition of San Antonio sportswriter Dan Cook's famous saying.

91 Number of points (91) that the Sacramento Kings surrendered during their 92-91 victory in Game 5 of the 2002 Conference Semifinals vs. the Los Angeles Lakers. After the Kings' Mike Bibby scored what would be the game winning shot, L.A.'s Kobe Bryant had a chance to win it with his own attempt. However, as he made his move, the Kings' Bobby Jackson bumped Bryant, causing the two to lose their balance. As Jackson fell, he grabbed Bryant's jersey. No foul was called before Bryant missed a jump shot to end the game. In Jackson's words, "I was thinking, 'Please miss. Please, please miss.' He's a great player. He doesn't miss many shots." He did this time and the Kings escaped with a victory.

92 Salary in the millions of dollars (9.2) for Sacramento King Kevin Martin during the 2008 season.

93 ARCO Arena record for most free throws (93) attempted by two teams in a regulation game. This record was set by the Sacramento Kings (43) vs. the Portland Trailblazers (50) on February 6, 1991.

94 Team leading number of blocks (94) collected by Vlade Divac during the Sacramento Kings 2001-02 Pacific Division championship campaign. The Kings ended the year with 375 rejections.

95 Number of points (95) scored by the Rochester Royals vs. the Boston Celtics during their November 13, 1948 matchup. Over 4,000 fans watched the Royals beat the Celtics 95-63 in the teams' first ever meeting.

96 Year ('96) that former Sacramento King Derek Smith passed away. During his NBA career, the former University of Louisville National Champion scored over 1,800 points. On August 10, 1996, Smith apparently died of a heart attack while on a cruise ship. Some people give Smith credit for inventing the high five! Smith was selected by Golden State in the 1982 NBA draft and played for the LA Clippers, Philadelphia 76ers, Boston Celtics, and Sacramento Kings. His son Nolan was a McDonald's All-American and signed with Duke, becoming a starter in 2008.

97 Year ('97) that the Kings struck a deal with the Sacramento City Council to keep the Kings in town. After owner Jim Thomas raised $20 million through an agreement on naming rights for ARCO Arena, the Council gave the Kings a $70 million loan. "The Sacramento Kings are going to stay in Sacramento," said Thomas. "It's been a long, hard road for a lot of us, but I'm pleased to be able to stand here today and say, 'We got it done.'"

98 Number of times (98) the Cleveland Cavaliers and the Sacramento Kings have faced off through the 2008 season. The Kings own a 51-47 record over the now LeBron James led team, having outscored them 10,310 to 10,259. Update: The Cavs last game vs. the Kings came on Friday the 13th in March of 2009. The Cavaliers walked away with a 126-123 OT win after James tossed in 51 points.

99 Cost in dollars ($99) for the Kings *Date Night with the Kings* package. The package includes two $25.50 tickets to the Kings game of your choice and two dinners at the Skyline Restaurant. Call for reservations by dialing (916) 928-8183.

100 Dollar amount (100) of the Victory Bond that 15-year-old Richard Paeth won for his Royals nickname submission during a 1946 contest to pick the Rochester mascot. Paeth beat out 500 other entries to win his Victory Bond. When the team moved to Kansas City, the team changed its name to the Kings because the cities baseball team was using the name Royals. Side note: In May of 1941, the first Series E U.S. Savings Bond was sold to President Franklin D. Roosevelt by Secretary of the Treasury Henry Morgenthau. The War Finance Committees sold a

total of $185.7 billion of securities. This selling achievement has not been matched since. By the end of World War II, 85 million Americans had bought War Bonds. Paeth's Bond matured in ten years. The Victory Bond was replaced with a Series EE bond in 1980.

Oscar Robinson

Sacramento Kings

"I played when I played, and played, I think, against the greatest players in the greatest time in the history of basketball."

— Oscar Robertson, NBA Hall of Famer

Chapter Two

The Big O

There is no player in the history of the Kings' franchise who epitomizes the game any better than the Oscar Robertson. Taken by the Cincinnati Royals as the number one pick in the 1960 NBA draft, Big O and his number 14 jersey had an immediate impact on the team and on the game. At 6'5" 205 pounds the former University of Cincinnati Bearcat showed speed and finesse and averaged 42.7 minutes per game as a rookie. He was not just in the game; he was the game, averaging 30.5 points and 10.1 rebounds per contest. He also led the league with an average of 9.7 assists per game, and he took home honors for Rookie of the Year.

As if averaging near a triple double your first year in the league wasn't impressive enough, Oscar took his game to the next level (which surprised everyone, not because they doubted his ability, but because it seemed impossible that there could be a level beyond the one he reached as a rookie). During his sophomore season of 1961-62, Robertson became the only player in the history of the NBA to average a triple-double (30.8 points, 11.4 assists, and 12.5 rebounds per game).

For the ten seasons that the "Horse" wore a Royals' jersey, he was consistent. His season low average for points-per-game was 24.7, in 1968, but that season he led the league in assists. His low average for assists per game was 8.1, his last season playing for Cincinnati. He would leave the organization with record upon record, both career and season. He would eventually earn a World title with the 1971 Milwaukee Bucks and go on to reach the Finals once more before retiring in 1974.

For many, however, no matter how great the triumphs were for Oscar on the court, it was his case in the courts that have left a more meaningful legacy on the game.

In 1970, the Oscar Robertson suit (so named since Oscar was the president of the union) was filed by the NBA Player's Association against the league. The anti-trust suit challenged the merger of the NBA and American Basketball Association, the college draft, and the NBA's reserve clause prohibiting free agency. The suit settled in 1976.

The result was that the NBA and ABA were allowed to merge, while the college draft remained intact. Drafted players were given the option of refusing to join the team that drafted them and reentering the draft one year later. Teams were no longer mandated to provide compensation when signing a free agent, which encouraged the signing of more free agents and led to higher salaries for players. The matter became known as "the Oscar Robertson Rule."

After leaving the game, Oscar returned to Cincinnati and became a successful businessman and an active community member involved in numerous charities and community activities. Although he no longer shoots hoop, he still follows it. Perhaps there will never be a triple threat greater than the Big O was during his years in the NBA . . . and, perhaps there has never been a better man to don an NBA uniform either.

Robertson's jersey was retired by the Kings as a reminder of his unbelievable play during his stint with the franchise.

The list of honors bestowed upon Oscar Robertson:

- Naismith Memorial Basketball Hall of Fame member (1980)
- NBA champion (1971, the year after being mysteriously dealt to Milwaukee)
- NBA MVP (1964)

- All-NBA 1st team (1961-69)
- Rookie of the Year (1961)
- NBA All-Star (1961-72)
- All-Star MVP (1961, 1964, 1969)
- Olympic gold medalist (1960)
- Named as one of the NBA's 50 Greatest Players.

101 Rebounds per game (10.1) by 2002 NBA All-Star Shareef Abdur-Rahim during the 2000 season. The 1997 first team NBA All-Rookie selection led the league in turnovers in 1999 (186). Abdur-Rahim had over 210 turnovers in each season from 1997-2003 excluding 1999. Fortunately, Shareef got a "handle" on things and in 2006 had only 108 TO while helping his Sacramento Kings to the NBA playoffs; his first ever playoff appearance. Also, the month and year (1/01) that Chris Webber scored 51 points and grabbed 26 rebounds in an overtime loss to the Indiana Pacers. It would take another 587 games before another King would record a 20/20 game. On January 30, 2008, Brad Miller would scorch the Charlotte Bobcats for 22 points and 20 rebounds in a 105-91 Kings' victory.

102 Kings/Royals franchise record for most rebounds (102) collected in an overtime game by the Cincinnati Royals vs. the Boston Celtics on November 8, 1957.

103 The average number of assists per game (10.3) recorded by NBA great Oscar Robertson. The Big O played for the Cincinnati Royals between 1960 and 1969 and, over the course of ten seasons, recorded 7,731 assists. His average assists per game is over two higher than Reggie Theus (8.1) who is second on the career per game list and his overall number of assists is more than *twice* as many as Sam Lacey, who has 3,563 total assists and is second on the all-time franchise list.

104 Number of points (104) scored by the Rochester Royals vs. Fort Wayne on January 16, 1952. Rochester won the game 104-71 making the 33 point win margin the fifth largest in the Rochester / Cincinnati era.

105 Points per game average (105) scored by the Kings vs. the Milwaukee Bucks during their 125 meetings through the 2008 season. The teams' last matchup on December 19, 2007, saw the Kings pull out a 102-89 victory in Milwaukee.

106 Number of points (106) surrendered by the Sacramento Kings vs. the Golden State Warriors during an April 16, 2002 matchup at home. The Kings won the game 120-106, and in doing so, set a franchise record for most wins in a season (61) and most home wins in a season (36). The 2001-02 Kings finished the year as Pacific Division Champions.

107 Points per game average (107) surrendered by the Kings versus the Los Angeles Lakers through the 2008 NBA season. The Kings have beaten the Lakers a total of 138 times in 388 meetings. Still, by average, each game is close. The Lakers score only four more points per game: 107-103.2.

108 Number of points (108) scored by the 1949-50 Rochester Royals during their home opener vs. the Sheboygan squad. The Royals won the game 108-75 in front of 3,500 fans.

109 Number of points (109) surrendered by the Kings vs. the Dallas Mavericks in Game Six of the 2003 Conference Semifinals. The Kings won the contest 115-109, forcing a Game Seven. A crowd of 17,317 gathered to watch the showdown, marking the 178th consecutive sell-out at ARCO. Commissioner David Stern was also in attendance. When he was announced at the game, the Kings' faithful booed him.

110 Number of points (110) scored by the Cincinnati Royals vs. Syracuse on October 26, 1957. This was the Royals first game in Cincinnati after moving from Rochester. The Royals won the game 110-100 in front of 5,122 fans.

111 Number of total wins (111) vs. the Boston Celtics through the 2008 season. The Kings have unfortunately lost on 169 occasions to the men in Green and White.

112 Franchise record for most field goals (112) attempted by a Kings/Royals' opponent during a postseason game. The Fort Wayne Pistons launched 112 shots on March 20, 1951.

113 Number of loses (113) compiled by Dick Motta during his stint with the Kings organization. His .298 winning percentage (48-113 record) is the fifth worst in Kings' franchise history.

114 Number of points (114) scored by the Sacramento Kings vs. the San Antonio Spurs on November 6, 1992 (Opening Night) at ARCO Arena in Head Coach Garry St. Jean's debut as the Kings' coach. The Kings won the game 114-106.

115 ARCO Arena record for most field goals (115) attempted by two teams during a half. The Kings (60) and the Golden State Warriors (55) set this record on March 5, 1989.

116 For NBA records purposes, month and day (11/6) in 1948 that the Kings' organization played their first official game. The home contest vs. Indianapolis ended with a Royals victory, 69-58. Over 4,000 fans attended the matchup.

117 Points (117) scored by the Golden State Warriors during a February 9, 1989 matchup in Sacramento. Fortunately for Kings fans, Sacramento scored 142 points of their own, making the combined total of 259 points an ARCO Arena record for most points scored during a regulation game.

118 Kings/Royals franchise record for most field goal attempts (118) tossed up during a postseason game. The record was posted at Philadelphia on March 24, 1967.

119 Points per game average (119) tallied by the 1962-63 Cincinnati Royals. Led by Oscar Robertson's 28.3 ppg average, the

Royals finished the season at 42-38. Once in the playoffs, Cincinnati fell to Boston 4-3 in the Division Finals.

120 The number of regular season wins (120) by the Kings in their back-to-back Pacific Division championships. During the 2001-02 season, the Kings posted a 61-21 record, their best winning percentage since 1948-49, and won their first division championship in 23 years. The Kings rolled over the Jazz (3-1) and the Mavericks (4-1) in the playoffs before losing in the Conference championship (3-4) to the Lakers. The next season, the Kings posted a 59-23 record and beat the Jazz in the playoffs (4-1). They were unable to beat the Mavericks for the second straight season, losing in the Conference semifinals in seven games.

121 ARCO Arena record for most rebounds (121) collected by two teams in a single game. The record was set by the Kings (64) and the Golden State Warriors (57) on March 5, 1989.

122 The number of points (122) scored by the Sacramento Kings vs. the Golden State Warriors on March 18, 2008. The Kings won the contest 122-105 as Kevin Martin led all scorers with 34 points on 13 of 22 from the field. Even though the game was over with the score being lopsided, Coach Reggie Theus took a timeout with 33 ticks left on the clock. Said Stephen Jackson of the Warriors, "I just take it as disrespect. That's just being cocky and showing off. That's just disrespectful." No love loss between these Bay Area rivals.

123 Number of points (123) scored by Joe McNamee during his 1951 season with the Rochester Royals. McNamee added another 33 points in 13 games played that postseason for the Royals. McNamee only played two seasons in the NBA, but won his ring in 1951 with Rochester.

124 Number of points (124) scored by the Kansas City Kings vs. the Portland Trailblazers on December 12, 1979. The Kings won the game 124-85, making the 39 point difference the fourth largest win margin in the Kansas City/Sacramento era.

125 Field goal percentage (.125) of Rochester's Bobby Wanzer during the 1952 NBA All-Star game on 1 of 8 shooting from the field.

The game was played at the Boston Garden as Wanzer's West club lost to the East 108-91. This was Wanzer's first All-Star contest.

126 Retail cost in dollars (126) of the Air Jordan 10 (X) Original (OG) shoes that were released in 1995. The black/dark concord and metallic silver basketball shoes were nickname the "Sacramento Kings" because of the regional release and color scheme.

127 Number of points (127) scored by the Kansas City-Omaha Royals vs. Atlanta on October 12, 1971. This was the Royals first game in KC after moving from Cincinnati. The Royals won the game 127-113 in front of 5,124 fans.

128 Number of points (128) scored by the Washington Bullets vs. the Kansas City Kings on January 26, 1979. Kansas City scored 142 points of their own, making the Kings total the seventh most points scored in a single game during the Kansas City/Sacramento era.

129 Number of points (129) scored by the New York Knicks vs. the Kansas City Kings on December 8, 1979. Kansas City scored 145 points of their own, making the Kings total the third most points scored in a single game during the Kansas City/Sacramento era.

130 Number of points (130) scored by the Royals vs. Detroit on New Year's Eve 1957. The Royals won the game 130-96 making the 34 point win margin the second largest in the Rochester/Cincinnati era.

131 Total number of minutes (131) played by three time All-NBA second team selection Bobby Wanzer during his five All-Star contests. From 1952 to 1956, Wanzer logged in 46 points, tallied 17 assists and rebounds, and shot .395 from the field during his All-Star appearances.

132 Number of field goals (132) made on 335 attempts by the Kings' Quincy Douby during his sophomore season with the Kings in 2008. Douby's salary that year was a cool $1.3 million.

133 Number of career starts (133) for Bobby Jackson through the 2007-08 season. Before being traded back to the Kings in 2008, Jackson

made stops with the Kings, Denver Nuggets, Minnesota Timberwolves, Memphis Grizzlies, New Orleans/Oklahoma City Hornets, New Orleans Hornets, and Houston Rockets.

134 Number of points (134) scored by the Sacramento Kings vs. the Golden State Warriors during the Kings 1987-88 home opener. Sacramento won the game 134-106 giving new head coach and Hall of Famer Bill Russell his first win of the season. Otis Thorpe led all scorers by dropping 31 points on the Warriors.

135 Kings/Royals record for most points (135) scored during a regulation postseason game vs. Boston on March 28, 1963. By halftime, the Royals dropped 74 points on the Celtics.

136 Dismal three point field goal percentage (.136) for the Kings' big man, Corliss Williamson, on six of 44 from behind the arc. In all fairness to the former NCAA All-American, Williamson didn't get $6.5 million in salary last year for his play behind the trey line. His game is played in the paint. In 2008, the former Arkansas Razorback collected 221 boards down low.

137 Kings/Royals record for most points (137) scored in an overtime playoff game. The feat was recorded vs. Dallas on May 10, 2003 in double overtime.

138 The number of games (138) played by the Sacramento Kings organization vs. the Chicago Bulls through the 2008 season. Even with the Bulls' six world titles, the Kings hold a winning record over Chi-town with a 71-67 posting.

139 Points (139) scored by the Sacramento Kings vs. the Dallas Mavericks on December 29, 1992. The Kings won the game 139-81 and recorded a franchise record for largest win margin at 58 points.

140 Team leading points per game average (14.0) by Bob Davies during the 1949-50 Rochester Royals season. Davies finished the year with 895 total points scored.

141 Points per game average (14.1) of Harold "Happy" Hairston during his 1965-66 campaign with the Cincinnati Royals. This was his second of four seasons with the club. The 6'7" forward also played for the Pistons and the Lakers during his career and won a World title in 1972 with LA. After retiring, Hairston started the Happy Hairston Youth Foundation to help less advantaged kids with college scholarships.

142 Franchise record for most points (142) surrendered by a Kings/Royals defense during a postseason game. The Celtics lit it up at the Boston Gardens on April 10, 1963.

143 Estimated number of points (143) that Cuttino Mobley scored by driving to the paint per 100 possessions during the 2004-05 season with the Kings. This estimation was calculated by Ed Peterson at www.82Games.com.

144 Personal fouls (144) committed by Chris Webber during his 2004-05 season with the Kings. That year, C-Webb was disqualified three times. Through the 2008 season, the former Michigan star was whistled for an even 2,700 fouls.

145 Height in inches (14.5) of the *Guidecraft* Sacramento Kings Step Stool for children. The stool helps your little ones get to hard to reach places. The stool displays the team's colors and logo.

146 Field goal attempts (146) credited to former Duke star and two time NCAA National Champion Bobby Hurley during his 1993-94 rookie season with the Sacramento Kings. Hurley only managed 19 games that year because of a December automobile accident. Hurley's vehicle was struck by a drunk driver and as a result Hurley was thrown from his truck, sustaining life threatening injuries. Hurley worked back and through rehab was able to play another four seasons in the NBA. One of the greatest college guards ever, Hurley's #11 jersey was retired by the Dukies in 1993.

147 Total rebounds (147) snagged by Win Wilfong during his 1960-61 season with the Cincinnati Royals; his last season in the NBA. Win was a winner, claiming a World title with the 1958 St. Louis Hawks.

148 ARCO Arena record for most points (148) scored by two teams in a half, set by the Sacramento Kings vs. the Golden State Warriors on January 21, 1989.

149 Number of points (149) scored by the Cincinnati Royals vs. the New York Knicks in their March 5, 1966 matchup. The Royals won the game 149-145 while scoring a season high 149 points in front of 10,023 fans.

150 Three point field goal percentage (.150) for Shareef Abdur-Rahim on 3 of 20 from the arc during his 2007 campaign with the Kings. Besides the 2008 season when Shareef only played in six contests, the 20 threes attempted in 2007 was his career low in attempts from behind the trey line.

151 Number of free throws (151) made by Wayman Tisdale and Anthony Bonner during their 1992 season with the Kings. Tisdale shot 151 of 198 from the line while Bonner made 151 of 241 free tosses.

152 Points per game average (15.2) for Hall of Fame inductee Bobby Wanzer during six NBA postseasons. Wanzer, a five time NBA All-Star, was a member of the 1951 World Champion Rochester Royals where he averaged 12.5 points in 14 playoff games. On a separate note: Wanzer was the first player in NBA history to ever shoot over 90% from the charity stripe. In 1952, Wanzer shot .904 from the line after connecting on 377 of 417 free throws.

153 The number of total rebounds (153) snagged by Anthony Peeler and the number of turnovers (153) given up by Peja Stojakovic during the Kings' 2003-04 season.

154 Combined number of points (154) scored by the Rochester Royals and the New York Knicks on April 21, 1951 in Game 7 of the 1951 NBA Finals. As all Kings fans know, Rochester won the game 79-75 for the organization's one and only NBA title.

155 Number of free throws (155) made by Rochester Royal Jack McMahon during his 1953 season with the Royals. McMahon would

later become a successful coach in the NBA, ABA, and American Basketball League.

156 Free throw attempts (156) by Art Spoelstra during his 1955 rookie season with the Rochester Royals. That year, Spoelstra scored 426 points and helped lead the Royals to the postseason. This would be Spoelstra's only playoff appearance.

157 The number of free throws (157) made by Billy Owens and the number of three pointers (157) attempted by Sarunas Marciulionis during their 1996 season with the Kings.

158 Number of turnovers (158) by both Chris Webber and Vlade Divac during the Kings' 2001-02 season. Doug Christie led all Kings in turnovers that year with 164 mistakes.

159 Total number of wins (159) collected by former Kings' Head Coach Garry St. Jean during his five seasons in Sacramento. St. Jean compiled a .402 winning percentage from 1993-97 after going 159-236.

160 Three point attempts (160) by Sacramento's Ricky Berry during his 1989 season with the Kings. This would be Berry's only season in the NBA. After a solid rookie season and just before his 25th birthday, Berry was found dead from a self-inflicted gunshot wound on August 14, 1989.

161 Total points (161) scored between the Sacramento Kings and the Orlando Magic during their January 21, 2006 meeting. The Kings lost the game 83-78 in overtime. Sacramento scored only 28 points in the final 29 minutes of play which included the third and fourth quarters and the five minute overtime. This was the first time in the NBA shot clock era that a team was held to fewer than 30 points in the second half during an overtime game.

162 Mitch Richmond's 1995-96 *Fleer* trading card number (162). The NBA endorsed card displays Richmond in a black Kings' uni, pushing the rock up the court.

163 Points per game (16.3) by Arnie Risen during the 1950-51 season. Risen, who played in 66 of the team's 68 regular season games, accounted for approximately 20% of the team's total offensive output. He also averaged 12 rebounds per game and 2.4 assists per contest, all well above his career averages, and led the Rochester Royals to the franchise's first and only NBA title.

164 Number of three point attempts (164) by Sacramento's Spud Webb and the number of defensive rebounds (164) pulled down by Walt Williams during their 1994 season with the Kings.

165 Ticket cost in dollars (165) for the best seats in the house at ARCO Arena for the Kings' 2008-09 season. These almost-on-the-court seats cost $7,260 for a full season plan.

166 Points per game average (16.6) by Sacramento's Wayman Tisdale during his 1992 season with the Kings. Tisdale scored a total of 1,195 points in 72 games and popped in 522 field goals for SAC that year.

167 Team leading number of offensive rebounds (167) secured by fan favorite Brad Miller during his 2007-08 season with the Kings. Miller would pull down a total of 681 boards on the year.

168 Points per game average (16.8) tallied by Rochester legend Maurice Stokes during his NBA Rookie of the Year season in 1956. The team didn't fair as well though, posting a 29-43 record and a third place finish in the Western Division.

169 Minutes (169) played during Jim Les' last season with Sacramento in 1993. The former Bradley University standout played in 321 career NBA games and scored 1,210 points. In 1991, Les led the NBA in three point field goal percentage on 71 of 154 from the arc.

170 Playing weight in pounds (170) of Sacramento's Kenny Smith during his 1988 season with the Kings. Smith and Franklin Edwards were the lightest players on the team at 170 pounds. This was Edward's last season in the NBA. That year, the former Cleveland State hooper scored 132 points for the Kings.

171 Number of personal fouls (171) committed by the Kings' John Salmons during his 2008 season in Sacramento. The 6'7" guard has been whistled for 793 fouls during his six season NBA career. Last year, Salmons made a cool $4.7 million in salary alone.

172 Total rebounds per game average (17.2) secured by Jerry Lucas during his three years of varsity play at Ohio State before being drafted by the Royals in the 1962 NBA draft.

173 Seating capacity (17.3) in the thousands at ARCO Arena, the home of the Sacramento Kings. The arena, which opened in 1988, cost $40 million to construct and increased the basketball seating capacity over the original ARCO Arena by about 7,000. Despite the improvement, the arena is the second smallest in the NBA in terms of capacity, just above the Amway Arena, the home of the Orlando Magic.

174 NBA league leading number of rebounds per game (17.4) by 2004 HOF inductee and three time NBA All-Star Maurice Stokes during the 1957 season. In 1956 he was selected as the NBA Rookie of the Year.

175 Number of wins (175) and loses (175) for the Kings vs. the Golden State Warriors after 350 contests through the 2008 NBA campaign. Although they both own a .500 record, the Kings have outscored the Warriors 106.9 to 106.7 per game.

176 The number of personal fouls (176) committed by Rodney McCray and the amount of points (176) scored by Sedric Toney during their 1990 season with the Kings. That season, McCray led the NBA in minutes played with 3,238 recorded while Toney played 32 games with the Kings and 32 with Atlanta.

177 Number of defensive rebounds (177) collected by two-time NBA World Champion Kenny Smith during his 1989 season with the Sacramento Kings. Smith played ten seasons in the NBA and was named to its All-Rookie team in 1988. The North Carolina graduate may be more recognizable to some for his post-NBA profession of studio analyst for *Turner Sports* on TNT and TBS.

178 Number of points (178) scored by the Sacramento Kings vs. the Detroit Pistons during the 1992 season. That year, the Pistons got the best of the Kings by recording a 2-0 record.

179 Number of field goals (179) made by former Villanova star Ed Pinckney during his 1988 season with the Sacramento Kings. Voted the Most Outstanding Player at the 1985 NCAA tournament for leading the Wildcats to an improbable NCAA title over Georgetown, Pinckney played 12 seasons in the league. He finished his career with 5,378 points and 3,952 rebounds.

180 Number of snakes (180) during the 2003 NBA season by guard Doug Christie. Christie was one of the premier defenders from 2001-04 with the Kings, earning a spot on the All-Defense team in each of those four seasons. He also led the league in steals during his first season in Sacramento with 183 snags in 2001.

181 Month and year (1/81) that Jeff Cohen was hired as Executive Vice President and General Manager of the Kings' organization. Cohen resigned after a 13 month stay.

182 Field goal percentage (.182) for the Kings David Cooke during his one season in the NBA. In 1986, Cooke would play 38 minutes and score nine points for Sacramento. Interestingly, Cooke was born in Sacramento, attended high school in Sacramento, and played pro ball in SAC.

183 Number of games (183) played between the Kings and the Houston Rockets through the 2008 season. Unfortunately for Sacramento fans, the Rockets own a 102-81 edge in the series.

ALL-STAR SBTN NUMBER

184 Number of blocks (184) by Kings legend Sam Lacey during his 1973-74 season with the KC-Omaha Kings. Lacey, who played a majority of his career with the Kings/Royals organization, is one of a handful of NBA athletes to record 100 steals and blocks in six consecutive seasons. Others are Dr. J, Ben Wallace, Hakeem Olajuwon, and David Robinson.

185 Month and year (1/85) that Joseph Benvenuti, Gregg and Frank Lukenbill, Stephen H. Cippa, Bob A. Cook, and Frank McCormick petitioned the NBA Board of Governors for permission to move the team from Kansas City to Sacramento.

186 Total number of rebounds (186) collected by Sacramento's Duane Causwell during his 1994 season with the Kings. Causwell played eleven seasons in the NBA after a stellar career at Temple.

187 Defensive rebounds (187) secured by the Kings' Corliss Williamson during his 1997 campaign with Sacramento. Also, the number of assists (187) dealt out by Billy Owens during the same year.

188 Total number of rebounds (188) secured by Hedo Turkoglu during the 2002-03 season with the Kings. That season, Hedo banked $1.3 million in salary.

189 Number of shooting fouls (189) committed by Mikki Moore during his 2008 season with the Kings. Trying to draw fouls on the defensive end is why Moore committed those shooting fouls. Still, he was able to draw 51 offensive fouls.

190 Number of free throw attempts (190) by the Kings' Bonzi Wells during the 2006 season. Wells hit 129 of those freebies for a .679 average from the line.

191 Team leading number of rebounds per game average (19.1) during a career by Kings legend Jerry Lucas. The 1980 Hall of Fame inductee led the Kings organization to four playoff appearances during his stay with the Cincinnati Royals from 1964-70.

192 Seasonal team high number of three point field goals (192) made by Mike Bibby during the 2005-06 season. That year, Bibby jacked up 497 attempts for a .386 percentage.

193 Number of defensive rebounds (193) grabbed and personal fouls (193) committed by Spud Webb during the 1991-92 Kings' season.

The 5'6" guard started 77 games for Sacramento that season and dropped a career high 1,231 points.

194 Number of times (194) that the Kings and Seattle Supersonics met before the Sonics jumped town and left for Oklahoma City following the 2008 season. During their meetings, the Kings averaged over 106 points per game.

195 Points (195) scored by the Chicago Bulls and the New Jersey Nets in head-to-head games vs. the Sacramento Kings during the 2008 NBA season. The Kings split with Chicago and dropped a 2-0 record on New Jersey during that season.

196 Total number of points (196) scored by the Sacramento Kings and the Phoenix Suns during the Kings' November 4, 1994 season home opener. The Kings won the game 107-89. Mitch Richmond led all scorers by pumping in 20 points.

197 Number of field goals (197) made by Gerald "Crash" Wallace during his three seasons with the Kings from 2002-04. The former University of Alabama star was the Kings' 25th overall selection during the 2001 NBA draft. Before enrolling at Bama, Wallace was selected to the McDonald's All-American team out of Childersburg, Alabama.

198 Month and year (1/98) that the Maloof family of Albuquerque, New Mexico, purchased a minority partnership in the Sacramento Kings squad. One year later, the Maloof family bought controlling interest in the team. The NBA Board of Governors approved the ownership transfer on May 7, 1999 and appointed Joe Maloof to the Board. The official date of the ownership transaction took place on July 1, 1999.

199 The 1995-96 *SkyBox* basketball card number (199) of Bobby Hurley. The Sacramento Kings' card displays Hurley dribbling to his left with a crowd of fans in the background looking on. The card's estimated worth is $2.95.

200 Total number of points (200) scored by the Sacramento Kings and the Toronto Raptors during their November 9, 2004 matchup. The Kings won the game 108-92, giving the Kings their first victory of the season. This was also the Kings home opener. Brad Miller and C-Webb led all scorers by tossing in 21 points each.

Mitch Richmond

Awards and Honors

All-Star Games
1993
1994
1995
1996
1997
1998

Rookie of the Year
1988-89

All-Star Game MVP
1994-95

All-Rookie 1st Team
1988-89

All-NBA
1993-94 2nd Team
1994-95 2nd Team
1995-96 3rd Team
1996-97 2nd Team
1997-98 3rd Team

NBA World Champion
2001-02

Olympic Gold Medalist
1996 Atlanta Games

Olympic Bronze Medalist
1988 Seoul Games

Kansas State University Retired Jersey

"Mitch is without a doubt one of the greatest athletes to ever play for the Sacramento Kings."

— *Geoff Petrie, Kings President of Basketball Operations*

Chapter Three

Mitch Richmond

Through the 2008 season, Mitch Richmond is one of only four players in NBA history to average at least 21 points per game in his first ten seasons in the league. Seven of those seasons were with Sacramento. This is one of many reasons why the Sacramento Kings decided to retire Richmond's #2 jersey.

On December 5, 2003, the Kings hosted the Minnesota Timberwolves at ARCO Arena and made Richmond the first player during the Sacramento era to have his number retired by the Kings' franchise. Not many fans will argue Richmond deserved such an honor. Although not all of Richmond's accomplishments happened in Sacramento, the organization chose to honor the scope of his career.

A career that started at Moberly Junior College in Missouri and progressed to a two year stint at Kansas State University where Richmond became the fifth overall selection in the 1988 NBA draft by the Golden State Warriors. Richmond played in Golden State for three years becoming part of the "Run TMC" club with Tim Hardaway and Chris Mullen. Richmond averaged just over 22 points per game and earned NBA Rookie of the Year honors in the process.

During the 1991-92 season, Richmond was traded to the Kings and immediately found a home. Like Nate Archibald in Kansas City before him, Richmond became the first legitimate star during the Sacramento era. Richmond ranks ninth overall in most games played by a King, fifth in minutes played, third in field goals made and attempted, second in three pointers made and attempted and ironically, first in turnovers.

Notwithstanding the last statistic, the Kings' organization and fans love Richmond and what he brought to ARCO. "Mitch is without a doubt one of the greatest athletes to ever play for the Sacramento Kings," said Kings President of Basketball Operations Geoff Petrie. "He was a consummate competitor, a clutch shooter and an all around great player who carried the colors for the Kings through some very difficult times. It's a great honor for the organization and for myself, personally, to participate in the celebration of his contribution to the Kings over the years. We're all deeply appreciative of his overall excellence. We'll always remember Mitch's efforts with the fondest of memories."

His career résumé reads like a proven veteran:

Six time NBA All-Star
1988-1989 NBA Rookie of the Year
1994-1995 NBA All-Star Game MVP
Five time All-NBA selection
1996 Olympic gold medalist
2002 NBA World Champion

Richmond's final career statistics read:

976 Career Games Played
902 Career Games Started
3,398 Assists
3,801 Rebounds
1,211 Steals
1,326 Three Point Field Goals Made
20,497 Points Scored

21 Points Per Game Average

The only question now is when will Mitch Richmond be invited to the Naismith Basketball Hall of Fame?

201 Points per game average (20.1) by the Kings' Antoine Carr during the 1990-91 season. Carr collected this team leading average after tossing in 626 field goals and popping in 295 shots from the charity line.

202 The total number of games (202) played by Maurice Stokes in his three seasons of basketball with the Rochester and Cincinnati Royals. The number two draft pick of 1955 out of St. Francis, Stokes made an immediate impact on the organization, averaging 16.8 points and 16.3 rebounds per game during his 67 game rookie season, good enough for Rookie of theYear honors. He continued his impressive career through both the 1956 and 1957 seasons, compiling a line of 202 games played, 16.4 points, and 17.3 rebounds per game.

203 Personal fouls (203) compiled by Mike Woodson during his 1982-83 season with the Kansas City Kings. That year, Woodson averaged 18.2 points per game. He is the current coach of the Atlanta Hawks and has a World Championship title as an assistant coach of the 2004 Detroit Pistons.

204 Month and day (2/04) in 1987 that the Kings scored only four points in the first quarter of a 128-92 loss to the Lakers. This was the fewest points scored by a team in the first quarter since the shot clock was introduced in 1954.

205 Playing weight (205) in pounds for the "Donut" Oscar Robertson during his illustrious career. The Hall of Famer was selected as the first overall selection during the 1960 NBA draft.

206 Number of assists (206) handed out by Vinny Del Negro during his 1989 season with the Sacramento Kings. Born in Springfield,

Massachusetts (home of the Hall of Fame), Del Negro made a mark for himself under Coach Jim Valvano at NC State his senior year by being selected to the All-ACC team. He was selected in the second round of the 1988 NBA draft and played 12 seasons in the league; finishing with 7,038 points. In 1994 *USA Today* named him "Most Caring Athlete."

207 Number of offensive rebounds (207) secured by Brian Grant during his 1995 season with the Kings. Grant played for five NBA teams during his career, but before entering the league, Grant was a two-time Midwest Collegiate Conference Player of the Year with Xavier.

208 Number of games (208) missed by Kings' players during the 2007-08 season. The reasons the games were missed range from surgery on knees to the flu.

209 ARCO Arena record for most field goals (209) attempted by two teams in a single game. This record was set by the Sacramento Kings (108) vs. the Golden State Warriors (101) on March 5, 1989.

210 Number of points (210) scored by the Kings organization vs. the Waterloo Hawks during their two meetings. The Rochester Royals outscored the Hawks 210-166 while posting a 2-0 record.

211 Points per game average (21.1) by the Kings' Shareef Abdur-Rahim during his one year at California. Abdur-Rahim was named NBA's #1 Good Guy by the *Sporting News* after funding the Reef House through his Atlanta based Future Foundation.

212 Points per game average (21.2) by the Kings' Peja Stojakovic during his 2002 season in Sacramento. Peja tossed in 547 field goals in helping lead the Kings to their first ever Pacific Division title.

213 Steals per game average (2.13) by Sacramento's Ron Artest during his 2006-07 NBA campaign. Artest was named the NBA Defensive Player of the Year in 2004 and All-Defensive First Team during his first season with the Kings in 2005-06.

214 Seat number (214) on the baseline of Section C at the Madison Square Garden for the March 20, 2009 matchup of the Kings vs. the Knicks costs $119 through www.stubhub.com in September of 2008.

215 The number of points (215) scored by the Kings and the Indiana Pacers during head-to-head games in the 2007-08 season. The clubs split their two matches that year.

216 The number of points (216) scored by the Miami Heat and the Toronto Raptors during games with the Kings in the 2008 season. Although the two clubs outscored Sacramento 432-403, the Kings were able to record a 2-2 record against those opponents.

217 Media Box (217) at ARCO Arena that has been reserved and designated as media seating. A portion of the scorer's table and Media Boxes 218 and 221 are also reserved for media.

218 Number of points (218) scored by Billy Owens during his partial season with the Kings in 1996. Owens was the third overall selection of the 1991 NBA draft after a stellar college career. In 1992 he was named to the first team All-Rookie club based on the 1,141 points, 639 rebounds, and 65 blocks he posted.

219 Team leading points per game average (21.9) posted by the Kings' Mitch Richmond during the 1993 season. That year, Richmond played in 45 games and shot 371 of 782 from the field. He was also selected to the All-Star game for the first time in his career, but could not participate because of an injury.

220 Number of points (220) scored by Gerald Wallace during his sophomore season with the Kings in 2003. Wallace, the 25th overall selection in the 2001 NBA draft out of the University of Alabama, lasted three seasons with the Kings before making his way to Charlotte.

221 The number of points (221) tallied by the Sacramento Kings vs. the Charlotte Bobcats during the 2007-08 season. The Kings walked away from that season series with a 2-0 record after outscoring the Bobcats 221-206.

222 Number of points (222) scored by the Kings and the Atlanta Hawks in their two games during the 1993 season. The teams split their two meetings as well.

223 Month and day (2/23) in 2000 that Chris Webber recorded a 20/20 game vs. the Atlanta Hawks by snagging 20 boards and scoring 28 points.

224 Number of field goals (224) made and number of assists (224) dished out by Brad Miller during the 2006-07 Kings' season. Also, the number of defensive boards (224) snagged by Mike Bibby the same season.

225 Number of three-point field goals (225) tossed up by Mitch Richmond during the 1995-96 season with the Kings. Richmond, who played the first three years of his career with Golden State and wrapped up his career in Washington and Los Angeles, is one of only nine Kings players to have their number retired. Other greats who have had their jersey numbers put to rest include Chris Webber, Vlade Divac, Nate Archibald, Bob Davies, Maurice Stokes, Oscar Robertson, Jack Twyman, and Sam Lacey. All of these legends played in either Rochester, Cincinnati, Kansas City, or Sacramento. The Sacramento Kings did retire one additional number, number six, the sixth man, for the fans in Sacramento.

226 Number of player games (226) lost to injury or illness by the Sacramento Kings club during the 1993-94 season. This was the third highest total in the NBA that year. The Kings utilized 20 different starting rotations over the season.

227 Personal fouls (227) assessed to the Kings Shareef Abdur-Rahim during Sacramento's 2006 NBA season. Only Brad Miller had more hacks that season with 234 whistles.

228 Month and day (2/28) in 2007 that the Kings' Mike Bibby tied a franchise record for most three pointers made in a half vs. Charlotte by canning six threes.

229 Number of minutes (229) played by the Kings' Lawrence Funderburke during the 2002-03 season. Funderburke might not have had too much time for balling that year. The former Ohio State star has always been busy with school. He has a degree from OSU, an MBA from the University of Phoenix, and has completed executive education programs at Stanford and Columbia.

230 Number of points (230) produced by the Kings vs. the Atlanta Hawks during the 2008 season and the number of points (230) scored by the Kings vs. the New York Knicks during the same season. The Kings compiled a 3-1 record against these opponents that year.

231 Three point field goal percentage (.231) of Vlade Divac during his 2001-02 season with the Kings. Divac ended his NBA career with a .235 percentage while canning 100 treys.

232 Minutes played per game average (23.2) tallied by 1990 Sacramento King draft pick Anthony Bonner during his NBA career. Bonner played six seasons in the NBA with the Kings, New York Knicks, and Orlando Magic.

233 Three point percentage (.233) for forward/guard Lionel Simmons during his 1997 season with the Kings on 7 of 30 shooting from beyond the arc. Simmons finished his career with a .305 average from out deep.

234 Number of minutes (234) played by Sam Ranzino during his 1952 season with the Rochester Royals. Ranzino was selected as the eighth overall pick in the 1951 NBA draft out of North Carolina State University. He was inducted into the North Carolina Sports Hall of Fame in 1981.

235 Total number of points (235) scored by the Sacramento Kings and the Phoenix Suns during their November 6, 2005 matchup. The Kings won the game 118-117, giving the Kings their first W of the season. Peja Stojakovic led all scorers by tossing in 33 points.

236 Number of field goals (236) made by the Kings' Corliss Williamson during his 2006-07 season in Sacramento. Side note: In high school, Williamson was a three-time All-Conference and All-State selection and was named as the Gatorade National Player of the Year in 1991 and 1992.

237 Team leading points per game average (23.7) by Sacramento's Kevin Martin during the 2007-08 season. Martin finished the year with 1,443 total points.

238 Three point field goal percentage (.238) recorded by a non-shooter, Chris Webber, on 5 of 21 from behind the arc during the 2003 season. That year, Webber scored 1,542 points to lead the Kings.

239 Kings/Royals record for lowest field goal percentage (.239) posted by a franchise team in a postseason game. The record was unfortunately set vs. Fort Wayne on March 24, 1953 after the team shot 17 of 71 from the field.

240 The number of three pointers (240) sunk by Peja Stojakovic during the 2003-04 season. Stojakovic joined the Kings in 1996 and remained with the club until being dealt to the Pacers mid-way through the 2006 season. The 2003 season saw career and league bests for Peja in three pointers and free-throw percentage (.927). Stojakovic averaged three treys per game and led the team in scoring with 24.8 points per game.

241 Number of rebounds (241) secured by Sacramento King Joe Kleine during his 1989 season with Sacramento. Kleine ended his NBA career with 3,991 rebounds.

242 Team leading points per game average (24.2) collected by Peja Stojakovic during the 2004 NBA season. This average was second best in the league during the 2004 season.

243 Team leading number of personal fouls (243) committed by Shareef Abdur-Rahim during the Kings' 2007 season. Abdur-Rahim averaged three hacks a game that year.

244 Weight (244) in pounds of both Ron Artest and Brad Miller of the Sacramento Kings during their 2006-07 season. That year, the two combined for 1,884 points.

245 Assists per game average (24.5) compiled by the 2004-05 Sacramento Kings. Mike Bibby led the way that year with 6.8 assists a game.

246 Number of games (246) played by the Kansas City – Omaha Kings. Their overall record from 1973-75 was 113-133 for a .459 winning percentage.

247 Minutes played per game (24.7) by Kenny Thomas during the Kings' 2005-06 first-round playoff series. During the playoff push, Thomas averaged 5.8 points per game.

248 Points per game average (24.8) tallied by Sacramento Kings President of Operations Geoff Petrie during his first season as a player in the NBA with the Portland Trailblazers in 1971. Petrie was the first-ever pick by the Blazers in the 1970 draft.

249 Points per game average (24.9) for the Kings' Kevin Martin during his junior season at Western Carolina. That year, Martin ranked second nationally in scoring and won the Southern Conference scoring title. In three seasons at Western, Martin scored 1,838 points.

250 Number of children (250) served on a daily basis in the Kings' "Read to Achieve" program. The year-round NBA campaign reaches an estimated 50 million children a year and attempts to help young people develop a love for reading.

251 Free throw attempts (251) by both Olden Polynice and Corliss Williamson during their 1997 season with the Kings. Polynice drained 141 of his attempts while Corliss hit on 173 of his free shots.

252 Points per game average (25.2) compiled by Chris Webber during the 2001-02 Conference Semifinals. During the five game series, Webber popped in 126 points. The 25.2 ppg average ranks 13th in

franchise history for highest points per game average in a single playoff series.

253 Winning percentage (.253) recorded by the 1959-60 Cincinnati Royals after posting a 19-56 record. This was the second season in a row that the Royals would only record 19 wins on the year.

254 Number of total rebounds (254) collected by the Kings' John Salmons during his 2006-07 season with Sacramento. The former University of Miami standout won a Pennsylvania state high school championship in 1997 while attending Plymouth-Whitemarsh High School.

255 Ticket cost in dollars (25.5) for each seat in sections 207-210 and 219-222 at ARCO Arena for the Kings' 2008-09 season. For season tickets in these sections, plan on paying a reasonable $1,122.

256 Last page (256) in the Sacramento Kings 2003-04 Media Guide to mention Franchise History. On page 257, the guide starts to list the team's All-Time roster. On the cover of the guide, the team boasts "Back-to-Back Pacific Division Champions."

257 Number of field goals (257) posted by Darius Songaila during his 2005 season with the Kings. That year, the former Wake Forest standout scored 608 points. This would be his last season in SAC before playing the 2006 NBA campaign with Chicago.

258 The number of defensive rebounds (258) secured by Billy Owens during his 1997 season in Sacramento. Owens was the third overall selection of the 1991 NBA draft after a stellar college career. In 1992 he was named to the first team All-Rookie club based on the 1,141 points, 639 rebounds, and 65 blocks he posted.

259 Number of minutes (259) played by Scot Pollard during his initial season with the Kings in 1998-99. "Samurai Scot" has one World Championship ring with the 2008 Boston Celtics.

260 Number of offensive rebounds (260) pulled down by former King LaSalle Thompson during the 1983-84 NBA season. This ranks sixth on the most offensive rebounds per season list recorded by a King. The year before he arrived in SAC, Thompson led the NBA in true rebound percentage with 19.8 as a member of the Kansas City Kings club.

261 Number of career blocks (261) through the 2008 season by the Kings' Corliss Williamson. Maybe his most memorable block came during his senior year in high school at the King Cotton Tournament when his Russellville team defeated Jason Kidd. With time winding down, Kidd put up a potential game winner, only to be blocked by Williamson. Corliss was named MVP of the tourney.

262 The number of free throws (262) made on 309 attempts by Brad Miller during his 2008 season with the Kings. Miller played 72 games for the Kings that year and scored a total of 964 points.

263 Number of assists per game (26.3) by the 1982-83 Kansas City Kings. That year, the Kings attendance averaged 8,301 fans a game.

264 Winning percentage (.264) for the 1958-59 Cincinnati Royals. The Royals finished the regular season at 19-53 and did not make the playoff for the first time since moving from Rochester to Cincy.

265 Number of total rebounds (265) secured by Walt Williams during his 1993 rookie season with the Sacramento Kings. Williams averaged 17 ppg and scored 1,001 points that season en route to a second team NBA All-Rookie selection.

266 Number of games (266) coached by former Sacramento Kings' Assistant Coach Steve Fisher when he was head coach at the University of Michigan. Fisher coached in Sacramento from 1998-99 and is most famous for leading the Wolverines to three NCAA title games and winning one during his first year as head coach in Ann Arbor.

267 The number of defensive rebounds (267) snagged by Joe Meriweather during his 1981 season with the Kansas City Kings.

Meriweather played a total of ten seasons in the NBA with the Kings, Rockets, Hawks, Jazz, and Knicks. He scored a total of 5,439 points over those ten years.

268 Free throws (268) made by Eddie Johnson during his 1984 season with the Kansas City Kings. Johnson attempted 331 charity shots that year for a .810 average after clocking over 2,920 minutes played that season.

269 Number of total rebounds (269) secured by Ron Boone during the 1978 NBA season. The former Kansas City King made four ABA All-Star appearances and played 13 seasons of pro ball.

270 Minutes per game average (27.0) tallied by John Salmons during the 2006-07 season. The 6'7" guard touched the court a total of 2,135 minutes that season.

271 Cost ($27.1) for a copy of the book *The Story of the Sacramento Kings.* The cover displays a picture of Mike Bibby pulling up for a jump shot over San Antonio Spur Tony Parker. The book was released in July of 2006 and is directed at children, ages 9-12.

272 Assists per game (27.2) tallied by the 1983-84 Kansas City Kings. That year, over 370,000 fans saw the Kings in action.

273 The winning percentage (.273) of the Sacramento Kings during April of 2007. Unfortunately for Kings' fans, Sacramento only won three games that month and was outscored 1,173-1,234 by ten different teams combined.

274 Three point field goal percentage (.274) compiled by Spud Webb during his 1993 season with the Kings. Webb hit 37 of his 135 trey attempts that year. The former NBA dunk champion scored an even 1,000 points in 1993.

275 Kings/Royals franchise record for highest points per game average (27.5) in a single playoff series. The record was set by Chris Webber in the 2003 Conference Semifinals.

276 Month and year (2/76) that the Kansas City Kings played 12 contests. The Kings opened February of 1976 with a 117-109 victory over the LA Lakers before losing five in a row and finishing the month with a 4-8 record.

277 Month and year (2/77) that the Kansas City Kings played 11 contests. The Kings opened February of 1977 with a 97-86 win at Chicago. The Kings completed the month with a 5-6 record.

278 Minutes per game average (27.8) for Brian Skinner during the Sacramento Kings' 2005 season. The 6'9" forward scored over 2,630 points during his first ten seasons in the league after dropping 1,662 points during his four years at Baylor University.

279 Number of assists (279) dished out by Mitch Richmond during the Sacramento Kings' 1998 season. As a team, the Kings recorded 1,836 lend-a-hands that year. Also, 279 is the number of free throws made by Corliss Williamson during the same year.

280 Weight (280) in pounds for Vitaly Potapenko during his 2007 season with the Kings. "The Ukraine Train" and former Wright State standout was the heaviest player listed on the 2007 Kings' roster.

281 Average family size (2.81) in French Lick, Indiana according to the 2000 census. French Lick is the hometown of former Sacramento Kings' coach Jerry Reynolds.

282 Number of points (282) scored by Frank "Pep" Saul during his 1951 season with the World Champion Rochester Royals. Although never an NBA All-Star, Pep did collect four world titles: one in Rochester and three with the Minneapolis Lakers.

283 Team leading points per game average (28.3) compiled by Oscar Robertson during his 1963 campaign in Cincinnati. The team finished in third place in the Eastern Division after recording a 42-38 record. The Royals did make the playoffs and lost a nail-biter series to Boston 4 games to 3 including a decisive Game 7, 142-131.

284 ARCO Arena record for most points (284) scored by two teams in a double overtime game, set by the Sacramento Kings vs. the Golden State Warriors on March 31, 1992.

285 Cost in the millions ($285) for the Palms hotel and casino located in Las Vegas. The Maloof family, owners of the Sacramento Kings, bought the 42-story tower which houses 447 guestrooms and opened for business on November 15, 2001. The hotspot was featured on *MTV*'s Real World and is known for their award winning restaurants, nightlife, and entertainment.

286 Field goal percentage (.286) of King reserve Maurice Taylor during his lone season with Sacramento in 2007. That year, the former University of Michigan Wolverine saw court time in 12 games. During his nine season NBA career, Taylor scored a total of 5,889 points.

287 Team leading number of assists (287) dished out by Bob Davies during his 1951 season with the world champion Rochester Royals. The team distributed 1,368 lend-a-hands that year.

288 Points per game average (28.8) compiled by Oscar Robertson during the 1961-62 Division Semifinals. During the four game series, Robertson chipped in 115 points. The 28.8 ppg average ranks fifth in franchise history for highest points per game average in a single playoff series.

289 Number of points (28.9) scored per 48 minutes by Peja Stojakovic during his 2004 NBA season. This average ranked sixth in the league that year.

290 Cost in dollars (29.0) for an "endless supply of hot, buttered popcorn" while seated in the ARCO Arena suites on game day during the 2007-08 season. Need a six-pack of soda to wash it down, plan on pulling out $15. Obviously, you can get these products for less at a grocery store. But how many times do you get to enjoy the Kings play from a suite at ARCO? It's worth it!

291 On April 3, 1986, the Sacramento Kings and the Los Angeles Lakers marked their (291st) meeting. The Lakers won that contest 135-105. The Kings most recent win vs. the Lakers was on December 9, 2008, 113-101. That game snapped an 8 game skid for the Kings and gave everyone in Sacramento something to cheer about. John Salmons and Francisco Garcia both tallied 21 points and Bobby Jackson added another 15. "It's probably our biggest win of the season, especially at home, since we've been struggling," Salmons said. "Hopefully we can grow from this." Going into the 2008-09 season, the Kings had beaten LA a total of 138 times.

292 Number of minutes (292) played by Kevin Gamble during his partial season with the Kings in 1996. Before entering the league, Gamble was part of a University of Iowa recruiting class that saw five members reach the NBA. Those players were Gamble, B.J. Armstrong, Les Jepsen, Ed Horton, and Roy Marble.

293 The average number of points (29.3) scored per game by Oscar Robertson during his ten seasons with the Cincinnati Royals. Robertson scored 22,009 points over 752 games and 33,088 minutes played. "The Horse" holds the franchise record in points and points per game, as well as numerous other categories.

294 Points per game average (29.4) compiled by Oscar Robertson during the 1962-63 Division Semifinals. During the five game series, Robertson chipped in 147 points. The 29.4 ppg average ranks fourth in franchise history for highest points per game average in a single playoff series.

295 Number of games (295) played vs. the Atlanta Hawks through the 2008 season. The Kings have won .515 of their games with the Hawks by securing a 152-143 record.

296 The number of turnovers (296) recorded by sure-hands Jason Williams during the Kings' 2000 season. Williams made up for it by compiling 589 assists that year.

297 Number of lend-a-hands (297) tallied by the Kings' Vlade Divac during his 2002 season with Sacramento. Divac was an instrumental part of the Kings' success that year as they compiled a 61-21 record. The veteran scored 888 points in 2002. On March 31, 2009, the Kings retired Divac's jersey. A fan favorite, Divac was humbled by the news of his pending jersey retirement. "It'll be very emotional and touching because it's a dream for every athlete to have their jersey retired after their career," Divac said. "I remember, obviously, the fans. They were great. The atmosphere we had in the locker room and on the court. The best six years of my career were here."

298 Winning percentage (.298) of Coach Dick Motta during his three year tour with the Kings' organization. His overall record with the Kings was a dismal 48-113. Motta may have an overall losing record in 25 years as a NBA head coach, but many argue he is deserving of a Hall of Fame bid. In 1971, Motta was voted NBA Coach of the Year and in 1978, he led his Washington Bullets to a NBA title. Not too shabby for a coach who came into the league having never tallied a minute of playing time in college or the pros.Motta's accomplishments:

- 935 career wins
- 1971 NBA Coach of the Year
- 1978 NBA Champion
- 14 seasons in the NBA playoffs

299 Month and year (2/99) that Sacramento's Chris Webber recorded a 20/20 game vs. the Phoenix Suns by snagging 20 boards and scoring 28 points. C-Webb recorded five 20 point/20 rebound games while playing with the Kings. In February of 2009, the Kings retired Webber's jersey and raised it to the rafters. "I'm just happy, humbled, excited—having every emotion you can think of, including a stomach that's tied up in knots," said Webber. "This was a really unexpected honor, one that I never expected to receive." Webber went on to say to the Kings' faithful, "I'm thankful that God brought me to Sacramento and let me be a King. You guys stood by me when the world left me for dead. I will always remember that."

Webber's accomplishments:

- 5 time NBA All-Star
- 5 times All-NBA
- All Rookie NBA
- 1994 NBA Ροοκιε οφ τηε Ψεαρ
- 1990-91 National High School player of the year
- NCAA Men's Division I Basketball All-American 1993
- NCAA All Tournament 1st Team (1992, 1993)
- Jerseys Retired: #44 Detroit Country Day School, #4 Kings
- 1999 NBA rebounding champ

300 Number of personal fouls (300) recorded by former Indiana University standout Tom Van Arsdale during his first full season with the Cincinnati Royals in 1969. Van Arsdale went on to become a three time NBA All-Star. During those three games, he chipped in 13 points. Van Arsdale was also listed on the first-team All-Rookie squad during his 1966 campaign.

Nate Archibald

Sacramento Kings

"Given a chance, I can play at this game."

— Nate Archibald, NBA Hall of Famer

Chapter Four

Tiny

Nathaniel "Tiny" Archibald was anything but. Although Nate only stood at 6'1" and weighed 150 pounds, he played bigger and stronger than his nickname suggested.

Inducted into the Naismith Hall of Fame as a player in 1991, Archibald spent 13 seasons in the NBA, carving up opponents with his quick hands, charitable ball distributing proficiency, and ball handling skills. So much so that he led the league with 910 assists and 2,719 points scored in 1973, becoming the first player to lead the league in these two categories during the same seasons.

Before being selected by the Cincinnati Royals in the second round of the 1970 NBA draft, Archibald grew up in the South Bronx, New York City and played his high school ball at DeWitt Clinton High School where he was an All-City selection in 1966. After graduation, Archibald enrolled at Arizona Western College before transferring to the University of Texas – El Paso to play under legendary coach Don Haskins.

At El Paso, Archibald impressed Haskins and became the team general even with his small stature. "I remember when he came to El Paso. I saw a little bitty guy . . . maybe 5-10, 135 pounds. His playground coach talked me into taking him. He was fun to coach. I didn't have to call timeouts when I had him, because I had a coach on the floor."

After arriving in Cincinnati, Archibald immediately made an impact on the NBA. Legendary NBA Hall of Famer and Kings' Coach Bob Cousy let Archibald run rampant. Within a short time, Nate became a one man show. He led the league in points scored per game at an amazing 34. He also led the league in minutes played per game with 46 and assists at 11.4. While playing with the Kings, Archibald made three NBA All-Star squads, was a four time All-NBA selection, and led the league in made free throws three times. His jersey #1 has been retired by the franchise.

In 1977, Archibald tore his Achilles tendon and became a trade pawn. With many thinking his career was over, the Boston Celtics took a chance on him. Although his stats weren't as gaudy in Boston, Archibald became a team player and got his championship ring with the 1980-81 Boston Celtics. While playing with the Celtics, Archibald was the 1981 NBA All-Star game MVP.

Archibald finished his career with 16,481 points, 6,476 assists, and 2,046 total rebounds, and was voted as one of the 50 Greatest Players of All Time, making "Tiny" anything but.

301 Minutes played per game (30.1) by Billy Owens during his 1998 season in Sacramento. Only Mitch Richmond and Corliss Williamson logged more minutes per game that year.

302 NBA league leading free throw attempts per game (30.2) tallied by the Kings during their 2006-07 season. The team also led the NBA in most free throws attempted with 2,473 tries. That same season, Mike Bibby posted his 4,000th career assist vs. Detroit on January 20, 2007.

303 Minutes played per game (30.3) by Hall of Famer Jack Twyman during his 1958 season with the Cincinnati Royals. That year,

Twyman led the league in field goal percentage and was voted to the NBA All-Star team where he scored 18 points in a losing effort. His West squad lost to the East 130-118.

304 Points per game average (30.4) compiled by Oscar Robertson during the 1963-64 Division Semifinals. During the five game series, Robertson chipped in 152 points. The 30.4 ppg average ranks third in franchise history for highest points per game average in a single playoff series.

305 Field goals (305) made by Tyus Edney during his 1996 season with the Sacramento Kings. Before making his move to the NBA, UCLA fans will remember Edney best for the move he made vs. the University of Missouri in the 1995 NCAA tournament. With UCLA down 74-73 with just under five seconds remaining, Edney dribbled coast to coast before banking a shot at the buzzer to help the Bruins move on in the tourney. That season, UCLA would win their 11th NCAA title.

306 Number of points (306) scored by the Rochester Royals during their 1951 Western Division Finals series vs. the Minneapolis Lakers. The Royals outscored the Lakers 306-287 during the 3-1 series win.

307 Month and day (3/07) in 2008 that the Sacramento Kings lost to the lowly Minnesota Timberwolves by a score of 111-103. Two days later, the Kings beat the mighty NBA Finals runner-up Los Angeles Lakers by a score of 114-113. Interestingly, the Kings led the Wolves in the standings by ten games and lost and trailed the Lakers by ten games and won.

308 Team leading points per game average (30.8) recorded by Oscar Robertson during his 1961-62 season in Cincinnati. Robertson also led the team in points scored with 2,432.

309 Minutes played per game (30.9) by Happy Hairston during his 1967 season with the Cincinnati Royals. Only Hall of Famers Oscar Robertson, Jerry Lucas, and Olympic gold medalist Adrian Smith logged more court time that year.

310 Number of defensive rebounds (310) collected by Sacramento's Mitch Richmond during his rookie season in the league. That year, Richmond took home the hardware for 1989 NBA Rookie of the Year.

311 Month and day (3/11) in 2005 that Mike Bibby drained a game winning shot vs. the LA Clippers. This was the second game in a row that Bibby hit a game winning shot. On March 8, Bibby also stopped Memphis 85-82.

312 Points per game average (31.2) for Jack Twyman during his 1960 season with the Royals. Although Twyman's average was second best in the NBA that year, the Royals still recorded a dismal 19-56 record. Fortunately for Royals' fans, Cincinnati used a territorial draft pick to select University of Cincinnati star Oscar Robertson the following season.

313 The number of points (313) scored while Mike Bibby, Cuttino Mobley, Peja Stojakovic, Darius Songaila, and Brian Skinner were on the court at the same time during the 2004-05 season. The five-man roster surrendered 323 points to their opponents while on the court together.

314 Points per game average (31.4) by NBA legend and Hall of Famer Oscar Robertson during his 1964 NBA MVP season. That season Robertson also averaged 9.9 rpg and 11 dishes per contest. However, even his 29.3 ppg average during the postseason couldn't help his Cincinnati Royals get by the Boston Celtics as the Royals lost 4-1 in the Eastern Division Finals.

315 Number of team leading fouls (315) committed by Connie Dierking during his 1968 season with the Cincinnati Royals. Dierking was the only player to get whistled at over 300 times. Over his NBA career, Connie got called for 2,075 personal fouls.

316 Total number of games (316) played by Lawrence Funderburke during his career in Sacramento. The Ohio State University graduate wrote the book titled *Hook Me Up, Playa!*. It was released in 2005 and exposes people targeting athletes for favors.

317 Month and day (3/17) in 2009 that the Sacramento Kings played in Atlanta. The St. Patrick's Day matchup was one of three holiday dates on the Kings' schedule during the 2008-09 NBA season. The other two contests were October 31 (Halloween) vs. Miami and April 12 (Easter Sunday) vs. San Antonio.

318 Month and year (3/18) in 2000 that the Sacramento Kings trailed the Clippers by 23 points before rallying to win 104-83 in Los Angeles.

319 Three-point field goal percentage (.319) by Walt Williams during the Kings' 1993 season. Williams hit 61 of his 191 three point attempts that year. His 191 launches were the most by any King player.

320 The number of games (320) played by the Kings vs. the Detroit Pistons through the 2008 season. The Kings own a slight lead in the series at 164-156 and have outscored the Motor City squad 33,117 to 32,941.

321 Basketball Association of America league leading number of assists (321) for 1970 Hall of Fame inductee Bob Davies during his 1948-49 season with the Royals. This would be the only time in Davies' career that he would lead the league in this category.

322 Three point field goal percentage (.322) by former Sacramento King Tyus Edney during his four seasons in the NBA. While in Sacramento, Edney launched 186 treys and hit 61 of them.

323 Team leading number of free throws (323) made by the Rochester Royals' Arnie Risen during the team's 1951 run to the world title. Risen attempted 440 charity shots that season.

324 Number of fouls (324) committed by Kansas City King Richard Washington during the 1977 and 1978 seasons. Over his NBA career, Washington was whistled at 1,179 times.

325 Month and day (3/25) in 2007 that Sacramento's Mike Bibby set a franchise record for most three pointers made in a game vs. the Phoenix Suns by drilling nine treys.

326 Month and day (3/26) in 2008 that the Sacramento Kings beat the Memphis Grizzlies 107-106, marking the 19th straight win over the Grizz in Sacramento. At that time, this was the second longest home winning streak for the Kings over a particular opponent. From 1997 to 2007, the Kings beat the Nuggets at home 20 straight times.

327 Number of turnovers (327) that former head coach Reggie Theus committed in 1986. Theus led the team in turnovers during the 1985, 1986, and 1987 seasons. Over his career, the former UNLV star turned the ball over 3,493 times. In all fairness, he handled the ball more than anyone else as well.

328 Month and day (3/28) in 1963 that Oscar Robertson scored 43 points vs. the Boston Celtics. This is a Kings' franchise record for most points scored in a playoff game. Robertson would tie this record by scoring another 43 points vs. the Celts on April 10, 1963.

329 Winning percentage (.329) of the 1998 Sacramento Kings after posting a 27-55 regular season record. The team finished fifth in the Pacific Division, and did not make the playoffs for the second consecutive season. That year's attendance at ARCO was 605,434 which ranked 25th in overall NBA attendance.

330 Water resistance distance (330) in feet that the Sacramento Kings Legend series watch is guaranteed to handle. The scratch resistant time piece displays the Kings' log and sells for $1,499.95.

331 *Upper Deck* basketball card number (331) of the Sacramento Kings' Predrag Stojakovic for his 1998-99 Rookie Card. *Beckett* priced the card in 2006 at $6.

332 Three point field goal percentage (.332) tallied by former University of Illinois star Nick Anderson during his 2000 season in Sacramento. In 1989, Anderson led his Fighting Illini to the NCAA Final

Four. As a junior at Illinois, he averaged 18 points, 2.5 blocks per game, and grabbed 7.9 boards per contest.

333 Field goal percentage (.333) for former University of Kansas Jayhawk Ryan Robertson during his one and only season in the NBA as part of the King's organization. Ryan managed to play in one contest during the 1999-2000 season and tallied 25 total minutes on the court while scoring five points. No matter the time, Robertson did something that many of us only dream of . . . he played in the NBA!

334 Number of points (334) scored by rookie Spencer Hawes during the 2007-08 season with the Kings. The tenth overall selection of the 2007 NBA draft from the University of Washington played 931 minutes and received hardwood time in 71 contests.

335 Number of turnovers (335) that Kansas City King Ray Williams committed in 1983. Williams only played for the Kings one season before making his way to Boston. Over his career, the former University of Minnesota star turned over the ball 2,099 times.

336 Defensive rebounds per game average (33.6) by the 2002-03 Sacramento Kings. This average was the best in the NBA that year. The Kings also ranked third in total rebounds per game with 44.5 boards a contest.

337 Minutes played per game (33.7) by Mike Bibby during the Kings' 2003 playoff run. That year, the Kings made a trip to the Western Conference Semis as Bibby recorded 12.7 ppg in 12 contests.

338 Number, according to the Kings' official website, www.nba.com/kings, of hugs (338) distributed by their mascot Slamson per game to Sacramento fans. Slamson was born in the fall of 1998. The feline is originally from Ngoro Ngoro Crater, Tanzania and attended Lion-el University.

339 Minutes played per game (33.9) by Sacramento King Doug Christie during the 2003 season. That year, Christie logged 2,711 minutes of court time in 80 games.

340 The single season franchise record for average points per game (34.0), held by Tiny Archibald. Nate Archibald, all 6'1" and 150 pounds of him, led the league in scoring and his average points per game is 2.6 points higher than Oscar Robertson, who holds the second place position (and seven others in the top ten) on the single season highest points per game record list.

341 Winning percentage (.341) for the 1993-94 Sacramento Kings after finishing with a dismal 28-54 record. A bright spot in the season was the selection of Mitch Richmond to the NBA West All-Star squad.

342 Number of games (342) played in a Sacramento Kings' uniform by Brad Miller through the 2008 season. Miller would start in 316 of those contests.

343 Number of seconds (34.3) left on the clock when Ron Artest hit a fade-away shot to put the Kings up for good in an April 7, 2006 matchup vs. the LA Clippers. The Kings won the game 96-93, thanks in part to Artest's play.

344 Three point field goal percentage (.344) posted by the Kings' Quincy Douby during his 2007-08 season in Sacramento. Douby jacked up 122 tries from behind the arc and made 42 of them.

345 The Kings' team value in the millions ($345) according to www.Forbes.com in 2005.

346 Number of games (346) played by Reggie Theus during his five seasons with the Kings' organization. During his time in Kansas City and Sacramento, Theus averaged 18.8 points per game.

347 Three point field goal percentage (.347) of former Syracuse star Billy Owens during his 1997 season with the Kings. Owens jacked up 72 treys and drained 25 of them that year.

348 Number of games (348) played by the Kings franchise vs. the Warriors franchise going into their March 18, 2008 matchup. Before

the Kings won that contest 122-105, the two teams had posted a 174-174 record vs. one another. The first game played between the two clubs was on November 11, 1948.

349 Field goal attempts (349) jacked up by Trevor Wilson during his 1994 season with the Sacramento Kings. That year, the former UCLA standout dropped 168 of those shots and scored 415 points for the Kings.

350 Number of games (350) coached by the legendary Bob Cousy during his stay with the Kings organization from 1969-1974. The Hall of Fame Celtics guard recorded a 141-209 record for a .403 winning percentage. During his first season at the helm, Cousy was a player/coach and inserted himself in the line-up seven times.

351 Number of blocked shots (351) tallied by the Kings' opponents during the 2003 season. Sacramento's defense compiled 457 blocks of their own that year.

352 Number of defensive rebounds (352) secured by the Kings' Ron Artest during his 2006-07 season in Sacramento. Side note: Artest is the only hooper in the NBA to be endorsed by Deutschland's k1x brand.

353 Number of three point field goals (3.53) per 48 minutes of playing time by Peja Stojakovic during his 2004 NBA season. This ranked second among all NBA players in the league that year.

354 Number of consecutive ticket sellouts (354) for the Sacramento Kings dating back to the 1999 season before the streak ended in 2007 at the Kings' home opener when 15,000 faithful showed.

355 Three point percentage (.355) recorded by Kings' opponents during the 2001 NBA season. That year, the Kings recorded a .354 percentage from the trey line themselves.

356 Three point percentage (.356) recorded by Sacramento King Francisco Garcia during his 2007 NBA season. Garcia launched 149 treys that year and drained 53.

357 Winning percentage (.357) of the Sacramento Kings during November of 2007. The Kings recorded a 5-9 record that month while being outscored 1,402-1,457.

358 Field goal attempts (358) by former Kansas Jayhawk Scot Pollard during his 2002 season with the Kings. Of those 358 shot attempts, Pollard connected on 197 of them.

359 Number of three point field goals (359) made on 1,037 attempts by the 1994-95 Sacramento Kings. Mitch Richmond led the club with 156 shots made from beyond the arc that year.

360 Minutes played per game (36.0) by Otis Thorpe during his 1987 season with the Kings. Only Reggie Theus saw more court time for the Kings that year when he logged 36.4 minutes per contest.

361 Number of blocks (361) posted by Lionel Simmons during his seven season NBA career with the Sacramento Kings. The "L-Train" was the seventh overall selection in the 1990 draft out of La Salle University.

362 Total number of minutes (362) played by Sacramento King Corliss Williamson during the 2006 NBA season. In limited court time, the Arkansas product scored 126 points for the Kings.

363 Field goal percentage (.363) on 103 of 284 shooting by Bobby Hurley during his 1995 sophomore season with the Kings. During his playing days at Duke, Hurley became the NCAA all-time assists leader and led Duke to back-to-back national championships. He also earned the Final Four Most Valuable Player honors in 1992. Hurley is the son of Bob Hurley Sr. one of the most accomplished high school coaches in the country. "Senior" has won 23 state titles in New Jersey with more on the way and over 900 games. Hurley Jr. ran the point for his dad on his 1989 team that went undefeated and ranked #1 in the nation.

364 Number of assists (364) handed out by Chris Webber during his 2003 season with the Sacramento Kings. Only Doug Christie recorded more lend-a-hands that year with 376.

365 Days (365) a year that the Kings; "Read to Achieve" program reaches young people. The year-round NBA campaign has been implemented by each and every team in the league and is used by an estimated 50 million kids a year.

366 Field goal percentage (.366) compiled by Ralph Sampson during his 1991 season with the Sacramento Kings. Side note: The Virginia native won the Naismith Award a record three times and was named the NBA All-Star MVP in 1985.

367 Three-point field goal percentage (.367) on 426 of 1,160 shooting recorded by the Sacramento Kings during their 2001-02 run to the Western Conference Finals.

368 Three point percentage (.368) recorded by Sacramento King Hedo Turkoglu during his 2002 NBA season. Hedo attempted 171 treys and netted 63 of those shots.

369 Points (369) scored by the LA Clippers vs. the Sacramento Kings during the 1998 season. During the teams' four game series that year, the Kings scored 364 points of their own.

370 Minutes (370) played by Hall of Famer Jerry Lucas during his first NBA postseason in 1964. During this ten game playoff run with the Cincinnati Royals, Lucas averaged 12.2 points per game while dishing out 34 assists.

371 Field goal percentage (.371) recorded by 6'3" guard Anthony Johnson during his 1998 season with the Kings on 226 of 609 shooting from the field. The former College of Charleston star may be best remembered for leading his Cougars to a NCAA first round victory over Maryland in 1997.

372 NBA league leading number of personal fouls (372) by 1981 Kansas City Kings first round draft selection Steve Johnson during his rookie season with the Kings. Johnson also led the NBA in fouls committed in 1987 with 340 hacks.

373 Three point percentage (.373) posted by the 2008 Sacramento Kings on 510 of 1,367 shooting from behind the trey-line. Amazingly, the Kings opponents also posted a .373 average from beyond the arc in 2008.

374 Three point percentage (.374) recorded by Danny Ainge on 108 of 289 shooting from behind the trey line in 1990. Ainge scored 1,342 points and dished out 453 assists for the Kings that year.

375 Shooting percentage (.375) of Jerome James during his only season with the Kings in 1999. The former Florida A&M standout was selected by the Kings as the 36th overall pick in the 1999 NBA draft. James wears a size 22 shoe and once dunked on an 11'4" basket while touring with the Harlem Globetrotters.

376 Number of pages (376) in the Sacramento Kings 2007-08 Media Guide. The guide gives Kings fans information on coaches, players, owners, staff, team records, playoff history, and much, much more.

377 Free throws (377) made on 523 attempts by Tom Van Arsdale during his 1971 season with the Cincinnati Royals. That year, Van Arsdale led the team with a 22.9 points per game average. The Royals didn't fair as well though, posting a 33-49 record.

378 Number of assists (378) dished out by Sam Lacey during his 1976 season with the Kansas City Kings. The previous season, Lacey would garner NBA All-Star status while lending out 428 help-outs.

379 Field goal percentage (.379) on 202 of 533 shooting from the hardwood by Rochester Royal rookie Bobby Wanzer during the 1949 season. The 1987 Hall of Fame inductee finished his career with a .393 shooting average.

380 Free throw attempts (380) by Cincinnati Royal Adrian Smith during his 1966-67 NBA campaign. Smith was the 85th overall selection in the 1958 NBA draft and became an NBA All-Star in 1966, when he scored a career high 1,470 points.

381 Number of points (381) scored by ABA and NBA All-Star Don Buse during his first season with the Kings in 1984. Known for his quick hands, Buse led the ABA in steals in 1976 with 346 snags and the NBA with 281 rips in 1977.

382 Number of defensive rebounds (382) snagged by Brad Miller in 2005. Miller led the team with 521 boards that year. Although Kenny Thomas tallied 535 rebounds that season, 308 of those were with the Philadelphia 76ers before being traded to Sacramento where he pulled down 227 boards in 26 games.

383 Field goal percentage (.383) tallied by Ron Artest during his 40 contests with the Sacramento Kings in 2006. With the Kings, the defensive handy-man collected 80 steals and grabbed 159 defensive rebounds.

384 Team leading number of free throws (384) made on 473 attempts by Bobby Wanzer during the 1951-52 Rochester Royals season. Wanzer finished the year with 1,020 total points scored and a 14.6 points per game average.

385 Field goal percentage (.385) of Rochester's Bobby Wanzer during the 1954 NBA All-Star game on 5 of 13 shooting from the field. The game was played at the Madison Square Garden as Wanzer's West club lost to the East 98-93. This was Wanzer's third All-Star contest.

386 Number of blocks (386) collected by the Kansas City Kings during the 1977 NBA season. The Kings looked to have a winning record all wrapped up until losing their last six games of the season, finishing at 40-42.

387 Number of free throw attempts (387) by the Kings former head coach, Reggie Theus, during his 1985 season with the Kansas City Kings. That year, Theus finished the season with a 16.4 points per game average.

388 Total number of minutes (388) played by Sacramento Kings Assistant Coach Kenny Natt during his few seasons in the NBA.

The former University of Louisiana-Monroe star was the 30th overall selection in the 1980 NBA draft by the Indiana Pacers.

389 Free throw attempts (389) by Antoine Carr during his 1991 season with the Sacramento Kings. Carr, known for wearing sunglasses on the court, led the team that season with 1,551 points and a 20.1 points per game average.

390 Team leading number of assists (390) dished out by Bob Davies during his 1951-52 NBA season. Davies not only led the team in lend-a-hands, but also topped the charts with a 16.2 points per game average.

391 Number of points (391) scored by Hedo Turkoglu during his rookie season with the Sacramento Kings in 2001. Hedo is the first Turkish born player in NBA history. The 16th overall pick in the 2000 NBA draft, Hedo was named to the second team All-Rookie squad.

392 Number of minutes (392) played by Royals' reserve William Holzman during his 1953 season in Rochester. This was the lowest amount of minutes played by any team member that season.

393 Field goal percentage (.393) of Walt Wesley during his rookie season with the Cincinnati Royals in 1967. Wesley played his college ball at the University of Kansas where he was an Associated Press third team All-American in 1966.

394 Number of games (394) won by Les Harrison while he was coach and owner of the Rochester Royals. He is the only coach who can claim a NBA title with the Kings' organization.

395 Number of wins (395) compiled by Coach Rick Adelman during his stint in Sacramento. He was able to secure five 50-plus win seasons with the Kings from 1998-2006.

396 Free throw attempts (396) by Cincinnati Royal Tom Van Arsdale during the 1972 season. The three time NBA All-Star hit 299 of those attempts while scoring 1,399 points that year.

397 Number of three-point field goals (397) attempted by Nick Anderson during his 1999-2000 season with the Kings. Anderson played in 800 games during his 13 season NBA career. From 1990-2002, Anderson would average 18.5 points per game including a career high 21.7 ppg average with the 1992 Orlando Magic.

398 Number of total rebounds (398) secured by Shareef Abdur-Rahim during his 2007 season in Sacramento. Shareef pulled down 276 defensive boards and fought for 122 offensive rebounds that year.

399 Cost in dollars ($399) for a Chris Webber autographed basketball at www.grandstandsports.com. The site has more King memorabilia for sale.

400 Field goal percentage (.400) by Rochester Royal Arnie Risen during his 1954 NBA All-Star appearance. In his third All-Star game, Risen would contribute eight points and hit four of his ten shot attempts.

Jack Twyman

Awards and Honors

All-Star Games
1957
1958
1959
1960
1962
1963

All-NBA
1959-60 2nd Team
1961-62 2nd Team

Naismith Memorial Basketball Hall of Fame Inductee
1983

Ohio Basketball Hall of Fame Inductee
2006

All-American
University of Cincinnati, 1955

"Show Twyman a little daylight and, boom, it's up and in."

— Red Auerbach, Legendary Boston Celtics' Coach

Chapter Five

Jack Twyman

Eleven years with one team doesn't happen in this league anymore. But in the 1950s and 1960s, loyalty to "royalty" in Cincinnati and Rochester was the norm. Hall of Famer Jack Twyman played in the NBA for 11 seasons, all with the Royals. A second round selection in the 1955 NBA draft, Twyman became a staple for the franchise, being voted to six All-Star squads and leading the Royals to six postseason appearances.

Before making the leap to the NBA, Twyman attended Central Catholic High School in Pittsburgh, Pennsylvania and then enrolled at the University of Cincinnati where he earned All-American honors in 1955 after averaging 17.8 points per game throughout his Bearcat career. In 90 college games, Twyman scored 1,598 points while knocking down 622 shots.

His scoring drive continued with the Cincinnati Royals, becoming the first player in Kings' franchise history to average over 30 points a game. He achieved this feat in 1960 after dropping in an unbelievable 870 field goals. Twyman also led the league in several different categories. In

1958, Twyman posted a .452 field goal percentage, 1959 saw him lead the NBA in field goal attempts with 1,691, and in 1960, Twyman recorded 598 free throws, proving that he truly was one of the most consistent players in the NBA.

After retiring from basketball in 1966, Twyman found himself as a television analyst for *The NBA* on ABC. New York Knicks' fans will best remember Twyman as the announcer who uttered the words, "I think we see Willis coming out." Moments before the 1970 NBA Finals Game 7, Twyman was doing a pre-game segment and noticed the legendary Willis Reed emerging from the tunnel towards the court. Reed's status for the game had been doubtful until Twyman announced to the world that Reed was on his way. Reed's presence propelled the Knicks to a 113-99 victory over the Lakers for their first NBA title.

Twyman made memorable moments on and off the court, but he will mostly be known as one of the greatest pure shooters and high scorers during the NBA's first two decades as a league.

401 Number of career assists (401) tallied by Reggie Theus during his college days at the University of Nevada–Las Vegas. From 1976-78, the Sacramento Kings' former head coach scored 1,177 points in Vegas.

402 Winning percentage (.402) of Head Coach Eric Musselman during his one season with the Sacramento franchise during the 2006-07 campaign. In three seasons at the helm of a NBA team, Musselman did not deliver a winning season. In two seasons with Golden State, he finished no higher than fourth in his division.

403 Number of assists (403) by Mike Bibby during his first season with the Kings during the 2002 NBA season. The former standout at the University of Arizona, Bibby led his Wildcats to the 1997 NCAA National Championship. Bibby is a member of Team Jordan, one of a select group of athletes hand picked by MJ himself to represent his clothing line.

404 Amount of dollars (4.04) in the millions that Mateen Cleaves signed for as part of his three year contract with the Sacramento Kings. Cleaves only played two seasons with the Kings before departing for Cleveland at the beginning of the 2003-04 season.

405 Ticket cost in dollars (40.5) for most seats in sections 201-204 and 213-216 at ARCO Arena for the Kings' 2008-09 season. For season tickets in these sections, plan on paying $1,782 a shot.

406 Field goal percentage (.406) of Travis Mays during his 1991 season with the Kings. Mays, a former standout at the University of Texas, played only one season in SAC before leaving for Atlanta. While in Sacramento, the 6'2" guard scored 915 points.

407 Three point field goal percentage (.407) on 127 of 312 shooting from downtown by Mitch Richmond during his 1994 season in Sacramento. Overall, this was second best on the team, as Jim Les converted on 8 of 18 treys for a .444 average.

408 Three point percentage (.408) tallied by the Kings' Sarunas Marciulionis during the 1996 NBA season on 64 of 157 shooting from beyond the arc. Marciulionis spent seven seasons in the league with one in Sacramento.

409 Cost ($40.9) for a Sacramento Kings *Hardwood Classic In the Paint* jersey by Majestic. This replica throw-back jersey is baby blue with a red and white stripe and an old Kings logo displayed over the heart.

410 Defensive rebounds per game average (4.10) for Mikki Moore during the 2008 NBA season. The Sacramento King averaged a total of six boards a game that season.

411 Field goal percentage (.411) compiled by Wayne Embry during his 1966 season with the Cincinnati Royals. Embry never won a NBA title with the Kings' organization, but he did hoist a World title with the Boston Celtics in 1968. Embry was enshrined into the Hall of Fame in

1999 as a contributor and was the first African-American NBA general manager, managing the Milwaukee Bucks from 1971-79.

412 Number of points (412) tallied by the Sacramento Kings vs. the Dallas Mavericks during the 1992 season. The Kings outscored the Mavs 412-389 while recording a 3-1 record vs. Dallas.

413 Number of blocks (413) secured by the Kings' opponents during the 2003-04 NBA season. That year, the Kings rejected 325 shots of their own.

414 The number of points (414) scored while Mike Bibby, Cuttino Mobley, Peja Stojakovic, Chris Webber, and Brad Miller were on the court at the same time during the 2004-05 season. The five-man roster surrendered 412 points to their opponents while on the court together.

415 Month and day (4/15) in 1999 that the Kings' Chris Webber recorded a 20/20 game vs. Seattle in overtime by snagging 21 rebounds and torching the Sonics for 26 points.

416 Month and day (4/16) in 2003 that Mike Bibby's consecutive free throws made streak ends at 51. The streak, which is a franchise record, ran from March 20 through April 16, 2003.

417 Rebounds per game average (41.7) by the Sacramento Kings during their 1992-93 campaign. Lionel Simmons led the charge with 7.2 boards a game.

418 Month and day (4/18) in 2004 that Sacramento set a franchise record 11 three-point field goals made vs. the Mavericks in Game 1 of their Western Conference first round matchup. Eleven days later they matched that record in their series clinching win over Dallas, 119-118.

419 Winning percentage (.419) of Coach Bobby Wanzer during his four seasons with the Kings' organization. His overall record with the Royals was a dismal 98-136.

420 Month and day (4/20) in 2002 that Mike Bibby played in his first ever NBA playoff contest. That day, Bibby recorded 20 points, four boards, and six lend-a-hands in 37 minutes of court time.

421 Field goal percentage (.421) by the Kings' Kenny Thomas during his 2007-08 season with Sacramento. The former University of New Mexico star slammed home 114 dunks in college and is one of only five Lobos to be selected as an All-American.

422 Points (422) scored by Rochester Royals' Jack Coleman while at the University of Louisville during the 1947-48 season. Louisville won the NAIB national title that year and played in the Olympic trials, losing to NCAA champion Kentucky. From 1946-49, Coleman scored 1,114 points, averaging a then-impressive 12.2 ppg while playing for the Cards.

423 Basketball Association of America league leading field goal percentage (.423) for 1998 Hall of Fame inductee Arnie Risen during his 1948-49 season with the Royals. This would be the only time in Risen's career that he would lead the league in this category.

424 Three point field goal percentage (.424) on 92 of 217 from behind the trey line by Cuttino Mobley during the Kings' 2005 season. That year, Mobley dropped 765 points.

425 Rebounds per game average (42.5) by Kings' opponents during the 1985-86 season. That year, Sacramento opponents pulled down 3,481 boards including 1,142 offensive rebounds.

426 Number of three point field goals (426) made by the 2001-02 Sacramento Kings during their run to the Conference Finals. The Kings would hold their opponents to just 386 treys made.

427 Number of field goals (427) made by Brian Grant during his 1996 season with the Kings. "The General" played three seasons in SAC before making his way north to Portland.

428 Rebounds per game average (42.8) by the Kings during the 1985-86 season. That year, Sacramento pulled down 3,512 boards including 1,135 offensive rebounds.

429 Field goal percentage (.429) on 9-21 shooting for Chris Webber vs. the Los Angeles Lakers in Game 7 of the 2002 Western Conference Finals. Webber scored 20 points and dished out 11 assists, but it was the Lakers' Shaquille O'Neal who led all scorers as LA won the contest 112-106 in overtime.

430 Minutes (430) played by Gerald Wallace during his 2002 season with the Kings. The Alabama native played 1,337 minutes for the Sacramento Kings before winding up in Charlotte with the Bobcats in 2004.

431 Winning percentage (.431) of the 1956-57 Rochester Royals. The team finished the season with a 31-41 record and a fourth place finish in the NBA Western Division. Although the team finished in the cellar, the Royals' Jack Twyman did make the 1957 All-Star team where he logged 17 minutes of playing time.

432 Field goal percentage (.432) tallied by the Kings' opponents during the 2001 NBA season. That year, the Kings recorded a .449 average of their own and scored 101.7 points per game. The number 432 is also the number of blocked shots recorded by the Kings during the same season.

433 Three point field goal percentage (.433) by Peja Stojakovic during his 2004 NBA season. This average ranked sixth in the league that year.

434 Field goal percentage (.434) of the Kings' Dahntay Jones during his 2007-08 season in Sacramento. The former Dukie found playing time in 25 contests and averaged 3.2 ppg.

435 Career winning percentage (.435) by KC-Omaha, Kansas City, and Sacramento Kings Coach Phil Johnson during his eight plus seasons in the league (the plus accounts for the one game he coached the

Chicago Bulls in 1982). Johnson earned 1975 NBA Coach of the Year honors after he led his Kings to a 44-38 record.

436 Total number of blocks (436) collected by the Sacramento Kings during the 1995-96 NBA season. That year, Brian Grant led the team with 103 rejections. Side note: Grant, a former Xavier star and First-team NBA All-Rookie selection, grew up in the same town as Civil War Union General Ulysses S. Grant.

437 Number of points (437) scored by former Sacramento King Bill Wennington during his 1990-91 season with the Kings. Wennington, a two-time Canadian Olympic athlete, is also a three-time NBA champion as a member of the Chicago Bulls.

438 Field goal percentage (.438) for former Sacramento King Danny Ainge during his 1989-90 season with the Kings. Ainge, a former Brigham Young star, also played Major League Baseball with the Toronto Blue Jays before going on to NBA stardom.

439 Field goal percentage (.439) for Bobby Jackson on 231 of 526 shooting from the hardwood during the 2001 season. That year, Jackson scored 566 points, helping the Kings to the fourth best record in the NBA at 55-27.

440 Field goal percentage (.440) for Ron Artest on 458 of 1,040 shooting from the floor during the 2006-07 season. That year, Artest averaged 18.8 points per game and led the team with 352 defensive rebounds.

441 Field goal percentage (.441) for 1988 Hall of Fame inductee Clyde Lovellette during his lone season with the Cincinnati Royals in 1958. The three time NBA All-Star scored 1,659 points for the Royals in 1958.

442 Last year ('44) and number of seasons (2) that the Rochester Pros played as an independent team. The Pros were a precursor to the Rochester Royals and the Kings' organization.

443 The average number of minutes (44.3) played per game by Oscar Robertson during the 1961-62 NBA season. Coming off a Rookie of the Year campaign that was, in and of itself, nothing short of phenomenal (30.5 points per game, 10.1 rebounds per game, and 9.7 assists per game), the Big O pulled off a feat that the greats like Jordan, Johnson, and Bird failed to do: he averaged a triple-double over the course of 79 games played, and he did it in only his second season in the league. Robertson averaged 30.8 points, 12.5 rebounds, and 11.4 assists per 44.3 minutes played.

444 Shooting percentage (.444) of the Kings' Bobby Jackson during his 2003-04 season in Sacramento. "Action Jackson," a crowd favorite, was awarded the NBA Sixth Man Award in 2003.

445 Number of points (445) scored by the Sacramento Kings vs. the Golden State Warriors during the 2006-07 season. The Kings posted a 1-3 record against the Warriors that year as Kevin Martin led the team with a 25.3 points per game average during those four contests.

446 Field goal percentage (.446) of both Mitch Richmond and Walt Williams during the 1995 NBA season. That year, Richmond hit 1,867 points while Williams scored 1,259 points for the Kings.

447 Field goal percentage (.447) of Mitch Richmond on 611 of 1,368 shooting from the field. Richmond led all Kings' scorers with 1,872 points that year.

448 Field goal percentage (.448) tallied by Peja Stojakovic during the 2000 NBA season. Peja tossed up 717 shots and drained 321 of them while scoring 877 points that year.

449 Field goal percentage (.449) compiled by Chris Webber during the 2005 NBA campaign. Webber jacked up 917 shots and netted 412 of them while scoring 978 points that year.

450 Number of assists (450) by Hall of Famer Nate Archibald during his rookie campaign with the Cincinnati Royals in 1971. Archibald finished his career with a seasonal high of 910 lend-a-hands

which he collected two years later. That was the same season in which he claimed a personal high 2,719 points.

451 Month and year (4/51) that the Rochester Royals beat the New York Knickerbockers for the franchise's lone NBA championship. The Royals earned $7,500 for winning the title.

452 League leading field goal percentage (.452) by six time All-Star and 1983 HOF inductee Jack Twyman during his 1958 season with the Cincinnati Royals. Twyman, a two time second team All-NBA selection, scored a total of 89 points on 68 field goal attempts during his All-Star appearances.

453 Number of points (453) scored by the Sacramento Kings during their 1999 first round playoff series with the Utah Jazz. The Kings lost the series 3 games to 2. That season, Chris Webber led all Kings' scorers with a 20 ppg average.

454 Team leading number of rebounds (454) secured by the Kings' Ron Artest during his 2007 NBA campaign. That year, Artest claimed 102 offensive boards and 352 defensive rebounds.

455 Field goal percentage (.455) tallied on 15 of 33 shooting from the field by Sacramento's Lionel Simmons during his only career playoff series. During the 1995-96 season, the Kings earned a spot in the Western Conference first round. Unfortunately for Kings' fans, the team lost to Seattle in four games.

456 Field goal percentage (.456) by #23 Kevin Martin during the Kings' 2008 season. Martin's game highs for the season were 48 points, ten rebounds, six assists, five steals, and one block. In September of last year, Martin participated in the Basketball Without Borders program in South Africa.

457 Field goal percentage (.457) of Gus Gerard during his 1980 season with the Kansas City Kings. Gerard was a 1976 ABA All-Star and received ABA All-Rookie honors in 1975. Gerard scored a total of 3,765 points during his pro career.

458 Winning percentage (.458) for the 1957-58 Cincinnati Royals. The Royals finished the regular season at 33-39 before falling to the Detroit Pistons 2-0 in the Western Division Semi-Finals.

459 Field goal percentage (.459) posted by the 2005 Sacramento Kings on 3,203 of 6,978 shooting from the hardwood. Amazingly, the Kings opponents also posted a .459 average from the field in 2005.

460 Winning percentage (.460) for the Sacramento Kings through the 2008 NBA campaign. From 1986 through 2008, the Kings compiled an 852-1,002 record.

461 NBA league leading three-point field goal percentage (.461) tossed in by Jim Les during his 1991 season with the Sacramento Kings club. The former Bradley University standout ended his NBA career with 1,210 points and made stops in Utah, Sacramento, Atlanta, and with the LA Clippers.

462 The number of games (462) played by Bob Davies in the BAA/NBA between 1948 and 1954. The "Harrisburg Houdini" led Seton Hall to 43 consecutive wins from 1939 until 1941 and, as an All-American guard, joined the US Navy during WWII. In seven seasons, Davies averaged 66 games played per season, averaged 14.2 points per games and just under five assists per contest. Davies was inducted into the Hall of Fame in 1970 and his #6 was retired by the team.

463 Winning percentage (.463) of first year Head Coach Reggie Theus during the 2007-08 season. The former NBA and University of Nevada – Las Vegas star recorded a 38-44 record for the Kings.

464 Field goal percentage (.464) posted by the 2008 Sacramento Kings on 3,043 of 6,558 shooting from the field. The Kings finished the year by scoring 8,408 points.

465 Shooting percentage (.465) for Dennis Hopson during his 1992 season with Sacramento. Hopson began the season with Chicago

before heading west. The previous year, Hopson won a NBA crown with the Bulls and is also Ohio State's all-time leading scorer.

466 Field goal percentage (.466) of NCAA Champion and former University of Arkansas star Corliss Williamson during his rookie season with the SAC Kings. The Kings chose the Russellville, Arkansas native as the 13th overall selection in the 1995 NBA draft. Williamson scored a total of 1,728 points for the Hogs in his three years at Fayetteville.

467 Number of field goals (467) made by 1979 Rookie of the Year selection Phil Ford of the Kansas City Kings. Ford, a former University of North Carolina standout, was the second overall pick in the 1978 NBA draft. Ford played seven seasons compiling 5,594 points and 3,083 assists.

468 Winning percentage (.468) for the Kings vs. the Dallas Mavericks through the 2008 season. The Mavs hold a 67-59 lead over the Kings, but have outscored them by an average of less than a point per game (106.1 to 105.3).

469 Number of losses (46.9) on January 8, 2008, that www.coolstandings.com projected the Kings would have by the end of the season. The Kings did a bit better and posted a 38-44 record that year.

470 Month and year (4/70) that Oscar Robertson was traded to the Milwaukee Bucks for Flynn Robinson and Charlie Paulk. In ten seasons with the Royals, he averaged 29.3 ppg, 10.3 assists, and 8.5 boards per game.

471 Winning percentage (.471) of the Sacramento Kings vs. the Indiana Pacers club after 68 contests through the 2008 NBA season. The Kings have averaged 103.8 points per game while giving up 104 per contest.

472 Shooting percentage (.472) recorded by Vlade Divac during the Kings' 2002 season. Divac attempted 716 shots and dropped in 338 of them that year. He was the sixth leading scorer on the team.

473 Total number of points (473) scored by Sacramento King Quincy Douby during his first two seasons with the team. The 19th overall selection in the 2006 NBA draft, Douby played his college ball at Rutgers where he helped lead his Scarlet Knights to a NIT final his freshman year.

474 Shooting percentage (.474) recorded by Shareef Abdur-Rahim during the Kings' 2007 season. Shareef attempted 654 shots and netted 310 of them that year. He was the fourth leading scorer on the team. Also, 474 is the number of points that Francisco Garcia scored that same season.

475 Month and year (4/75) that former Sacramento King Michael Stewart was born in CutqTrepiedStel, France. The 6'10" center played one season in Sacramento and contributed 375 points for the 1998 Kings.

476 The number of games (476) coached by Rochester Royal legendary coach Les Harrison. Between 1948 and 1954, Harrison led the Royals to a 295-181 record (.620 winning percentage) and an NBA championship in 1950-51. Harrison was also instrumental in the merger between the NBA and BAA and the introduction of the 24-second shot clock.

477 Seasonal team high number of three point field goals (477) attempted by Mitch Richmond during his 1996-97 season with Sacramento. That campaign, Richmond put in 204 shots from beyond the arc.

478 Number of field goal attempts (478) credited to Mike McGee during his 1988 season with Sacramento. McGee played only 37 games for the Kings during his career, but managed to find playing time in Los Angeles with the Lakers, in Atlanta, New Jersey, and with the Phoenix Suns during his nine seasons in the NBA. He has two NBA championship rings as part of the Lakers dynasty.

479 Shooting percentage (.479) of Doug Christie during the Kings' 2003 NBA season. The defensive-minded-baller jacked up 557 shots and busted 267 of them that year en route to 9.4 ppg average.

480 Field goal percentage (48.0) posted by Kevin Martin during his sophomore season in the league. In 2006 Martin logged 1,913 minutes of playing time and averaged 10.8 points per game.

481 Winning percentage (.481) of the 1966-67 Cincinnati Royals. The team finished the season with a 39-42 record and a third place finish in the NBA Eastern Division. The Royals lost in the Eastern Division Semis 3-1 to the Philadelphia Sixers.

482 Team leading career three-point field goal percentage (.482) by a Kings franchise player, recorded by Anthony Peeler in 2004. The former University of Missouri standout also led the NBA in three-point field goal percentage that season on 68 of 141 shots taken from behind the arc.

483 Field goal percentage (.483) recorded by Jimmy Walker during his 1976 season with the Kansas City Kings. Walker was a two time All-Star and scored 11,655 points during his career. Walker was also the father of former NBA star Jalen Rose. He passed away on July 2, 2007 from complications related to lung cancer.

484 Shooting percentage (.484) posted by the Kansas City Kings' Larry McNeill during his 1976 season with the Kings. The former Marquette University standout was drafted by the KC/Omaha Kings as the 25th overall selection in the 1973 NBA draft.

485 Field goal percentage (.485) tallied by Eddie Johnson during his 1984 NBA campaign. That year, the 6'7" forward scored a total of 1,794 points to lead all Kings' scorers.

486 Number of field goals (486) netted by Hall of Famer Tiny Archibald during his rookie season with the Cincinnati Royals in 1971. That year, Tiny scored 1,308 points for the Royals.

487 Free throw percentage (.487) recorded by Nick Anderson during the Kings' 2000 season. Anderson shot 76 charity shots and converted on 37 of them.

488 Winning percentage (.488) of Coach Ed Jucker during his two year stint with the Kings' organization in 1968 and 1969. His overall record with the Cincinnati Royals was 80-84.

489 Shooting percentage (.489) for Ollie Johnson on 218 of 446 from the field during his 1977 season with the Kansas City Kings. Johnson played ten seasons in the league. He is currently the Director of Athletics at the Community College of Philadelphia.

490 Field goal percentage (.490) of Lawrence Funderburke during his 1998 season in Sacramento. The Columbus, Ohio native played six seasons in SAC before playing his final NBA season in Chicago.

491 Combined points per game average (49.1) of Oscar Robertson and Jerry Lucas during the Cincinnati Royals' 1963-64 season. The duo also averaged 13.6 assists per game and 27.3 rebounds per game in their first season as teammates.

492 Number of free throw attempts (492) tossed up by Tom Van Arsdale during his 1970 season with the Cincinnati Royals. Van Arsdale hit 381 of those charity shots for a .744 average.

493 Field goal percentage (.493) of Oscar Robertson during the Cincinnati Royals' 1967 season. Not only was Robertson the team's leading scorer that year, his .493 average was also the best on the squad.

494 Number of points (494) scored by Bill Turner during the Cincinnati Royals' 1970 NBA campaign. The former University of Akron star had his jersey retired by the school. His #42 college number hangs in the James A. Rhodes Arena.

495 The number of free throw attempts (495) put up by Reggie Theus during his 1987 season with the Kings. Theus nailed 429 of those tosses and ended the season with 1,600 points; tops on the team.

496 Number of points (496) scored by Red Holzman during his 1951 season with the World Champion Rochester Royals. Holzman would end up spending five years in Rochester before finishing his career with the 1954 Milwaukee Hawks.

497 Three point attempts (497) launched by Mike Bibby during his 2006 season in Sacramento. Bibby nailed 192 of those treys and ended the season with over 1,700 points scored.

498 Number of points (498) scored by Scot Pollard during the Kings' 2001 season. Through the 2008 season, Pollard has scored an even 2,222 points during his NBA career.

499 Career field goal percentage (.499) tallied by Hall of Famer Jerry Lucas. "Luke" attempted 11,441 shots during his eleven seasons in the league. He hit 5,709 of those shots.

500 Winning percentage (.500) of the Rochester Royals after their only two meetings vs. the Sheboygan Redskins during the 1949-50 season. Both games were played during the first ten days of November, 1949. The Royals took the first game 108-75, but ten days later, the Redskins got revenge while defeating Rochester 97-87.

Maurice Stokes

Sacramento Kings

"Had things not turned out like they did there would've been a Royals' dynasty instead of the Celtics."

— Jack Twyman, NBA Hall of Famer and former teammate of Maurice Stokes

Chapter Six

Maurice Stokes

Maurice Stokes played only three seasons in the NBA. Some former players and NBA fans would argue that Stokes should not have been inducted into the Hall of Fame in 2004 based on his on-court achievements. Those individuals didn't know Stokes or what he stood for, the work he did for his community, and the love for the game he had.

Stokes played 202 NBA games, logged 7,544 minutes, averaged 16.4 points per game, and grabbed 3,492 boards throughout his short career. He led the league in total rebounds grabbed in 1957 and also rebounds per game in 1956. Stokes was a three time NBA All-Star and was selected as the 1956 NBA Rookie of the Year. Before turning pro, Stokes played for tiny St. Francis and earned a fourth place finish at the prestigious NIT while earning tournament MVP honors. He was also a third team Associated Press All-American before being selected by the Rochester Royals as the second overall pick in the 1955 NBA draft.

All the potential for a glorious and lengthy career came crashing to the floor on March 12, 1958. It was the last game of the regular season between the Royals and the Lakers. Stokes flipped over an opponent's shoulder and crashed into the ground head first becoming unconscious. When he awoke from being passed out, he continued to play. In fact, he joined his team for a three game playoff vs. the Pistons three days later.

After Game 1 of the Pistons series in which Stokes posted 15 boards and 12 points, Stokes became violently ill and fell into a paralyzed state, days later. Teammate Jack Twyman stepped in with his wife Carol to become Stokes' legal guardians. For 12 years, the Twyman's cared for Stokes as his speech, mobility, and strength improved. Unfortunately for humanity, Stokes died of a heart attack on April 6, 1970. He was 36 years old.

Before his death, Stokes accompanied Twyman to annual exhibition games and learned to type and paint, although his fingers and hands didn't always work the way he wanted them to. Maurice Stokes never gave in, he never quit working. He never quit on life and that along with his unbelievable play, sense of humor, and courage made him a perfect selection for the Naismith Hall of Fame.

Maurice Stokes:

NIT Most Valuable Player, 1955
NBA Rookie of the Year, 1956
Three time NBA All-Star, 1956-58
All-NBA Second Team, 1956-58
Naismith Hall of Fame, 2004

501 Field goal percentage (.501) by Keon Clark during his 2003 season with the Kings. In his lone season with SAC, Clark played in 80 games, started 11, and scored 536 points. The former UNLV Rebel suited up for five NBA seasons.

502 Shooting percentage (.502) of former Villanova star Ed Pinckney during the Kings' 1989 season. Pinckney attempted 446 shots and canned 224 of them en route to a 12.3 ppg average that year.

503 Month and year (5/03) that Bobby Jackson graced the cover of *Sports Illustrated*. The cover shows Jackson pushing the ball up the court and the headline reading, "Sacramento's Secret Formula: Bobby + Bibby = Perfect Point Guard."

504 Winning percentage (.504) of Coach Cotton Fitzsimmons during his six year stint with the Kings' organization. His overall record with the Kings was 248-244.

505 Number of three-point field goals (505) jacked up by Jason Williams during his 1999-2000 season with the Kings. This total ranks third on the all-time list of most treys put up in a season by a Kings player. The street-baller displays numerous tattoos including "White Boy" tattooed in Old English letters on his fingers.

506 Number of field goals (506) made by Danny Ainge during the 1990 season. Currently, Ainge is the General Manager and Executive Director of Basketball Operations for the Boston Celtics.

507 Number of points (507) scored by Jack McMahon during his rookie season with the Rochester Royals in 1953. McMahon, a former standout at St. John's, finished his NBA career with 4,237 points.

508 Number of total career loses (508) recorded by coach Rick Adelman through the 2008 season. The former Sacramento King coach has a 807-508 record with four NBA teams.

509 Field goal percentage (.509) by Wayman Tisdale during his 1993 season in Sacramento. That year, Tisdale led all King scorers with 1,263 points. The 28 year old played in 76 games while starting 75 of them.

510 Number of points (510) scored by Nate Archibald during his college playing days in El Paso. The prep star from New York, New York

made his way down south and ended his college play by averaging 23.2 points per game in three years.

511 Number of points (511) scored by Bill Calhoun during his 1951 season with the World Champion Rochester Royals. Calhoun was born, raised, and attended college in San Francisco before making the leap to the NBA where he would spend seven seasons.

512 Team leading number of defensive rebounds (512) brought down by Sacramento's Michael Smith during the 1997 NBA season. Smith added up 2,526 total minutes of playing time behind only Mitch Richmond (3,125) and Olden Polynice (2,893).

513 Free throw percentage (.513) posted by Kenny Thomas during the 2007 season. As a team, the Kings recorded a.765 average after knocking down 1,891 free throws on 2,473 attempts.

514 Number of points (514) scored by the Sacramento Kings vs. the Seattle Supersonics during the 1995 NBA season. Although the Sonics outscored the Kings 531-514, it was the Kings that tallied a 3-2 record in head-to-head.

515 Seasonal team high number of three point field goals (515) attempted by Mitch Richmond during his 1995-96 season with the Kings. That season, Richmond tossed in 225 threes.

516 Month and day (5/16) in 1984 that the Kings' Quincy Douby was born in Brooklyn, New York. He is the only Rutgers player to ever be drafted by the Kings.

517 Field goal attempts (517) by Sacramento's John Salmons during his 2006-07 season with the Kings. The 6'7" guard and former University of Miami standout scored 671 points that year while popping in 236 of his shots.

518 Field goal percentage (.518) and number of defensive rebounds (518) secured by LaSalle Thompson during the 1986 NBA

season. The former University of Texas standout scored 7,806 career points.

519 True shooting percentage (.519) posted by Darnell "Dr. Dunk" Hillman during his 1979 season with the Kansas City Kings. Known for his acrobatic dunks and oversized afro hair style, Hillman played 682 games in the NBA and ABA combined. It is rumored that a reporter once asked Hillman if he could jump and snag a quarter off the top of a backboard. Hillman confidently replied, "Put a $100 up there and see." The reporter declined.

520 The number of points (520) scored by the Sacramento Kings vs. the Golden State Warriors during the 1994 NBA season. Unfortunately for SAC fans, the Warriors scored 565 points of their own while compiling a 4-1 record vs. the Kings.

521 Number of shots (521) made by Scott Wedman during his 1977 season with the Kansas City Kings. Wedman attempted 1,133 shots that year and averaged 15.4 ppg. "The Invisible Hulk" represented the Kings in two All-Star games. A former University of Colorado standout, Wedman was used as a backup player for Larry Bird and Kevin McHale during Boston's 1984 and 1986 World Championship seasons. Wedman may always be remembered for coming off the bench in Game 1 of the 1985 Finals vs. the LA Lakers and hitting all 11 of his shot attempts including four treys in a 148-114 Celtic win.

522 Month and day (5/22) in 1994 that the Kings' organization unveiled the current logo and team colors. The colors changed from red, white, and blue to purple, black, and silver.

523 Free throw percentage (.523) credited to the Kings' Mark McNamara during his 1984-85 season with Kansas City. McNamara played in eight NBA seasons and found the court in 278 games. The former Cal Bear standout scored a total of 980 points during his career.

524 Field goal percentage (.524) of Sacramento's Brad Miller during the Kings' 2005 season. Miller tossed up 609 shots while

converting 319. In four seasons at Purdue, Miller jacked up shots in 128 college games.

525 Winning percentage (.525) of the 1962-63 Cincinnati Royals. The team finished the season with a 42-38 record and a third place finish in the NBA Eastern Division. The Royals lost in the Eastern Division Finals 4-3 to the Boston Celtics after beating the Syracuse Nationals 3-2 in the Eastern Division Semis.

526 Field goal attempts (526) by Sacramento King guard Bobby Jackson during his 2001 NBA season. Jackson hit 231 of those shots while scoring 566 points on the year.

527 NBA league leading field goal percentage (.527) recorded by former Ohio State University standout Jerry Lucas during his rookie season with the 1963-64 Cincinnati Royals.

528 True shooting percentage (.528) recorded by former Louisiana State University standout Jabari Smith during his rookie season with the Kings. Smith was drafted by the Kings in the second round of the 2000 NBA draft as the 45th overall selection. Currently, Smith plays in the Iranian Basketball Super League with Pardis Mottahed Qazvin BC.

529 Career free throw percentage (.529) of former Sacramento King Michael Smith. "The Animal" played his college ball at Providence and was the 35th overall pick in the 1994 NBA draft by the Sacramento Kings.

530 Number of three-point shots (530) tossed in by the 2007 Sacramento Kings. That year, the Kings jacked up 1,513 attempts to post a .350 average from behind the arc. Mike Bibby led the team with 173 treys.

531 Number of field goals (531) made by Bucky Bockhorn during his 1962 season with the Cincinnati Royals. Born Arlen Dale Bockhorn, "Bucky" may have the sweetest name in franchise history. Bockhorn played seven seasons in Cincinnati where he scored 5,430 career points.

532 Winning percentage (.532) for the Sacramento franchise vs. the New Orleans Hornets organization through the 2008 season. After 47 games, the Kings hold a 25-22 edge in head-to-head meetings.

533 Number of blocks (533) recorded by the Kings' opponents during the 1988 season. The Kings rejected 493 shots of their own that year, led by Jawann Oldham's 110 blocks. Oldham played one season in Sacramento and scored 297 points for the Kings.

534 Number of three point field goals (534) made by the Kings on 1,656 attempts for a .322 percentage during the 2000 season. Jon Barry led all Sacramento shooters with a .429 three point field goal average.

535 Number of points (535) scored by the Kansas City Kings vs. the Phoenix Suns during the 1976 season. The Kings were outscored by the Suns 542-535 but managed to win three of their five meetings that season.

536 Number of minutes (536) played by the Kings' Bobby Jackson during the 2005 season. Jackson found playing time in 25 games and scored 301 points that year.

537 The Kansas City – Omaha Kings winning percentage (.537) during the 1974-75 season. Coming off a 27-30 record the season before, coach Phil Johnson led the Kings to a 44-38 mark and a second place finish in the NBA Midwest Division. Even though the Kings lost to the Bulls in the Western Conference Semifinals, their efforts earned coach Johnson Coach of the Year honors.

538 The winning percentage (.538) for the Kings during the month of February in 2007. The Kings managed a 7-6 record that month while outscoring their opponents 1,332-1,310.

539 Team leading field goal percentage (.539) by Mike Peplowski during his 1994 rookie season with the Kings. Peplowski made 76 of his 141 shot attempts and scored 176 points for Sacramento that year.

540 Winning percentage (.540) of the 1999 Sacramento Kings after posting a 27-23 regular season record. The team finished third in the Pacific Division, and was bounced from the playoffs by the Utah Jazz in the Western Conference first round. That year's attendance at ARCO was 418,751 which ranked 15th in overall NBA attendance.

541 Field goal percentage (.541) of former Sacramento King Scot Pollard during his 1999 NBA campaign. Pollard attempted 61 shots that season and connected on 33 of them. Only teammate Lawrence Funderburke had a higher shooting percentage in that year.

542 Shooting percentage (.542) of former University of Oklahoma star Wayman Tisdale during his 1991 season with the Kings. That year, Tisdale logged 1,116 minutes of playing time and scored 660 points for the Kings.

543 Free throw attempts (543) by Otis Thorpe during the 1987 season. Thorpe drained 413 charity shots that year while being the second leading scorer on the team. The ever steady player ended his career after 17 seasons in the NBA.

544 Field goal percentage (.544) tallied by Reggie King (1981) and Olden Polynice (1995). Through the 2008 season, this ranks ninth on the Kings' all-time list for best field goal percentage posted in a single season.

545 Number of total rebounds (545) collected by NBA All-Star and 1994 Rookie of the Year Chris Webber during his first season with the Kings in 1999. That year, "C-Webb" led the NBA with a 13 rebounds per game average. Webber has always been the center of attention and now he commands *Center Court* - a restaurant opened by Webber in Sacramento, California that pays homage to NBA greats.

546 Number of strikeouts (546) tossed by Major League Baseball All-Star and former Princeton basketball and baseball star Chris Young through May 24, 2008. Young was offered a NBA contract to play for the Sacramento Kings in 2002 before turning it down to play baseball. Young currently plays for the San Diego Padres.

547 Field goals (547) made by Peja Stojakovic during the 2001-02 season. The former King attempted 1,130 shots that year and posted a 21.2 points per game average in 2,648 minutes of play.

548 Number of points (548) scored by the Sacramento Kings vs. the Golden State Warriors in 1991. The Kings outscored the Warriors by 26 points that season and posted a 3-2 record against the GSW.

549 Winning percentage (.549) of the 1982-83 Kansas City Kings' squad. The team finished the season with a 45-37 record and a second place finish in the NBA Midwest Division.

550 True shooting percentage (.550) of former Georgia Tech standout Jon Barry during his last season with the Sacramento Kings during the 2001 season. Jon, son of Hall of Famer Rick Barry, made plenty of stops around the league other than with the Kings during his career including setting up shop in Houston, Atlanta, LA, Milwaukee, Golden State, Denver, and Detroit.

551 Shooting percentage (.551) of Jerry Lucas on 555 of 1,007 from the field during his 1969 season with the Cincinnati Royals. Lucas recorded a field goal percentage over .500 on six different occasions during his career.

552 Team leading number of defensive rebounds (552) compiled by Sacramento's Brad Miller during the 2004 season. The two time World Championship bronze medalist (1998 Greece and 2006 Japan) finished the season with 743 total boards.

553 Number of field goals (553) made by Jimmy Walker during his 1974-75 season with the Kansas City-Omaha Kings. The 6'3" guard from Providence was the second leading scorer on the team that season behind Tiny Archibald's 2,170 points.

554 Seasonal team high number of three point field goals (554) attempted by Peja Stojakovic during his 2003-04 season with the Kings. That year, Peja drained 240 treys.

555 Number of points (555) scored by the Phoenix Suns vs. the Kansas City Kings during the 1983-84 season. The Kings scored 523 points of their own during the five game regular season series.

556 Number of minutes (556) played by the Kings' Greg Ostertag during his 2005 season in Sacramento. Before suiting up in the NBA, Ostertag was star at Duncanville High School in Texas. Ostertag (already a seven-footer at the time) led his squad to the 5A State title before leaving for Kansas where he helped the Jayhawks to two Final Four appearances.

557 Number of three point field goals (557) made by Sacramento Kings' opponents during the 2007 season. That year, the Kings drained 530 treys of their own, led by the 173 drained by Mike Bibby.

558 True shooting percentage (.558) by Mitch Richmond during his 1993 season. The former Kansas State star logged a .557 true shooting percentage during his 14 season career.

559 Field goal percentage (.559) tallied by Cincinnati Royals' Johnny Green during his 1969-70 NBA campaign. This percentage also led the league that year. Through the 2008 season, this ranks sixth on the Kings' all-time list for best field goal percentage posted in a single season.

560 Number of rebounds (560) secured by Wayman Tisdale during his 1994 season with the Kings. Tisdale also snagged 1,048 boards during his stay in Norman, Oklahoma as a member of the University of Oklahoma Sooners basketball program.

561 Number of shots (561) made by Corliss Williamson during the 1998 NBA season. Corliss ended the year as the second leading scorer on the Kings team with 1,401 points.

562 Free throw percentage (.562) on 141 of 251 shooting from the line by Olden Polynice during his 1997 season in Sacramento. Olden finished the year by scoring 1,025 points; third best on the team.

563 Winning percentage (.563) of the 1965-66 Cincinnati Royals. The team finished the season with a 45-35 record and a third place finish in the NBA Eastern Division. The Royals lost in the Eastern Division Semis 3-2 to the Boston Celtics.

564 NBA league leading true shooting percentage (.564) for the Royals' Arnie Johnson during the 1950-51 season. Johnson would finish the season with 639 points after shooting 185 of 403 from the field.

565 NBA league leading true shooting percentage (.565) for the Royals' Arnie Johnson during the 1951-52 season. Johnson would finish the season with 657 points after shooting 178 of 411 from the field.

566 Number of field goal attempts (566) recorded by Harold Pressley during his 1990 season with the Kings. Pressley, a former first round selection in the 1986 NBA draft, played four seasons in Sacramento and scored a total of 2,702 points during his pro career.

567 Number of field goal attempts (567) tossed up by Ricky Berry during his rookie season with the Kings in 1989. The former San Jose standout played one season in Sacramento and scored 706 points that year; fourth best on the team.

568 Total number of games (568) played by five time NBA All-Star Bobby Wanzer during his basketball career. The former Seton Hall standout played all nine seasons with the Rochester Royals.

569 Number of points (569) scored by Vinny Del Negro during his 1989 season with the Kings. The former NC State star is now the head coach of the Chicago Bulls.

570 Seasonal team high field goal percentage (.570) compiled by Matt Guokas during his 1972-73 season with the Kansas City/Omaha Kings. That year, Guokas tossed in 322 shots. This .570 shooting percentage was a career high for Guokas.

571 Winning percentage (.571) of the Rochester Royals during December of the 1948-49 season. That month, the Royals posted an 8-6 record while outscoring their opponents 1,166 to 1,154.

572 Number of steals (572) recorded by the Kings' opponents during the 2007 season. Sacramento snagged 671 steals of their own that year, led by Ron Artest's 149 take-aways.

573 Winning percentage (.573) of the 1979-80 Kansas City Kings' team. The squad finished the season with a 47-35 record and a second place finish in the NBA Midwest Division. The Kings lost in the Western Conference first round 2-1 to the Phoenix Suns.

574 Number of points (574) scored by Sacramento's Anthony Johnson during his 1998 rookie season with the Kings. Johnson was drafted in the second round of the 1997 draft by the Kings, but played only one season in Sacramento before being dealt to the Atlanta Hawks. Since that season, Johnson has played in Atlanta, Orlando, Cleveland, New Jersey, Indiana, and Dallas before making his way back to Sacramento in 2008 to finish the season with the Kings.

575 Three point attempts (575) by Francisco Garcia during his first three seasons in the league. Through the 2008 season, Garcia has hit 205 treys and scored 1,822 points.

576 True shooting percentage (.576) posted by Peja Stojakovic during the 2001 NBA season. That year, Peja dropped in 1,529 points to become the Kings' second leading point getter behind Chris Webber.

577 Shooting percentage (.577) tallied by Mikki Moore during his 2008 season with the Sacramento Kings. Through the 2007-08 season, Moore has recorded six seasons with a field goal percentage of over .500.

578 Total number of career rebounds (578) secured by Oscar Robertson during his postseason appearances with the Cincinnati Royals and the Milwaukee Bucks.

579 NBA league leading true shooting percentage (.579) recorded by Jerry Lucas during his 1963-64 season with the Cincinnati Royals. That year, Lucas was selected as NBA Rookie of the Year.

580 Shot attempts (580) by Walt Williams during his 1994 season with the Kings. That year, Williams dropped in 226 field goals for a total of 638 points in 1,356 minutes of court time.

581 Winning percentage (.581) of the Sacramento Kings in games decided by more than 11 points in 2006. In games that were decided by less than four points, the Kings recorded a .545 winning percentage.

582 Month and year (5/82) that Leon Karosen, H. Paul Rosenberg, and Robert Margolin became the three sole owners of the Kings' organization. However, three months later, three other businessmen joined the ownership team.

583 Number of points (583) scored by the Rochester Royals during their 1951 NBA Finals series vs. the New York Knickerbockers. The Royals won the series 4 games to 3.

584 Number of steals (584) that Mike Bibby recorded while wearing a Kings' uniform. The 584 snags ranks third in the Sacramento era.

585 Winning percentage (.585) of the 1978-79 Kansas City Kings. The squad finished the season with a 48-34 record and a first place finish in the NBA Midwest Division. The Kings lost in the Western Conference Semis 4-1 to the Phoenix Suns.

586 Month and year (5/86) that legendary Hall of Famer Willis Reed took over as assistant coach of the Sacramento Kings. Unfortunately for Kings' fans, Reed would resign from his duties on February 29, 1988 to accept the head coaching job with the New Jersey Nets. While in New Jersey, Reed would collect a 33-77 record.

587 Field goal percentage (.587) by Johnny Green during his 1970-71 season with the Cincinnati Royals. This percentage ranks fourth on the all-time field goal percentage list for Kings players.

588 True shooting percentage (.588) by Oscar Robertson during his 1963 season with the Cincinnati Royals. Robertson was the leading scorer on the team that year by dropping 2,264 points.

589 Free throw percentage (.589) on 116 of 197 charity shots made by Billy Owens during his 1998 season with the Kings. Owens was the third leading scorer on SAC's team during the 1997-98 campaign by scoring 818 points.

590 NBA league leading true shooting percentage (.590) recorded by Jerry Lucas during his 1968-69 season with the Cincinnati Royals. That year, Lucas was selected to the NBA All-Star team for the sixth time.

591 Number of field goal attempts (591) jacked up by Dennis Hopson during his 1992 season with the Kings. This would be Hopson's last year in the NBA after five seasons. Before putting on a pro uni, Hopson was a 1986-87 NCAA Associated Press second team All-American.

592 Number of field goal attempts (592) by Sacramento King Bobby Jackson during his 2004 season with the Kings. Jackson drained 263 of those shots and scored 689 points on the year.

593 Free throw percentage (.593) surrendered by the Cincinnati Royals vs. the San Francisco Warriors during the teams' March 20, 1970 matchup. The Royals posted a .721 percentage and was led by Tom Van Arsdale's 32 points that day.

594 True shooting percentage (.594) recorded by Matt Guokas Jr. during his first season with the KC-Omaha Kings in 1973. Guokas became half of the first father-son duo to win NBA titles as players. His father, Matt Guokas Sr., was a member of the 1947 Philadelphia Warriors team that won it all and Jr. claimed his World title in 1967 with the

Philadelphia 76ers. Although Guokas Sr. officially played with the Warriors team that participated in the BAA, the NBA recognizes the BAA stats from 1947. HOF inductee Rick Barry and son Brent Barry matched this feat by winning NBA Championships in 1975 and 2005 respectively.

595 Number of field goal attempts (595) tossed up by Tom Hawkins during his 1963-64 season with the Cincinnati Royals. Before entering the NBA, Hawkins became the first African-American player to play at Notre Dame.

596 Free throw percentage (.596) tallied by Pete Chilcutt during his 1993-94 season in Sacramento. Chilcutt dropped in 31 of his 52 attempts that year for the Kings.

597 Effective field goal percentage (.597) drained by Doug Christie during his 2005 season with the Kings on open uncontested shots. That year Christie scored 226 points on 83 of 204 shooting from the field.

598 The number of total rebounds (598) pulled down by Brian Grant during his 1995 season with the Kings. That year, Grant collected 207 offensive boards and cleaned the glass on the defensive end 391 times.

599 Field goal attempts (599) by Flynn Robinson during his 1967 season with the Cincinnati Royals. Robinson had two stints with the Royals; from 1967-68 and again in 1971. Over his career, Robinson played on five NBA teams and one ABA squad.

600 Field goal percentage (.600) by former Kansas City and Sacramento King Otis Thorpe during his 1984-85 season with the organization. This percentage ranks third on the all-time field goal percentage list recorded by a King.

Sacramento Kings Franchise History

Rochester Royals
1945-57

Cincinnati Royals
1957-72

Kansas City-Omaha Kings
1972-75

Kansas City Kings
1975-85

Sacramento Kings
1985-present

Home arenas

Edgerton Park Arena (1945-1955)
Rochester War Memorial (1955-1957)
Cincinnati Gardens (1957-1972)
Kansas City Municipal Auditorium (1972-1974)
Omaha Civic Auditorium (1972-1978)
Kemper Arena (1974-1985)
ARCO Arena I (1985-1988)
ARCO Arena II (1988-present)

"Our community is great. They support us through all the good times and bad, and always show great passion and support for their team."

— Kevin Martin, Sacramento Kings

Chapter Seven

East to West: The Most Traveled Team in the NBA

Founded in 1945 by owner/head coach Les Harrison and his brother Jack, the Sacramento Kings' franchise started on the right coast as the Rochester Royals while part of the National Basketball League. Led by Bob Davies, the Royals won the NBL championship in 1946 and 1947 before moving to the National Basketball Association in 1948.

The Royals won their only NBA title in 1951 and called Rochester home for a total of 12 years. While in New York, the Royals would feature nine future Hall of Famers: Al Cervi, Bob Davies, Les Harrison, Red Holzman, Arnie Risen, Jack Twyman, Alex Hannum, Maurice Stokes, and Bobby Wanzer. The franchise also included a future Hollywood actor and Major League Baseball player named Chuck Connors and future Football Hall of Famer Otto Graham.

In 1957, the Harrison brothers moved the team to Cincinnati where financial success did not follow them. Despite making the playoffs, the team lost a reported $25,000 and the Harrison brothers reacted by attempting to move the team back to Rochester. The NBA balked however because Rochester wasn't considered a major market. The Harrison's sold out and the team stayed in Cincinnati.

Despite the presence of Oscar Robertson, Jerry Lucas, and Bob Cousy, and seven post season appearances, the Royals moved to Kansas City/Omaha to escape a declining fan base. In its third season, the newly named Kings made the playoffs in 1975. However, the next season the team would call Kansas City its sole home. In ten seasons as the Kansas City Kings, the team would make four playoff appearances before moving to Sacramento in 1985.

The team received a renewed sense of purpose once in Sacramento. For eight straight seasons the franchise would make the postseason with players like Chris Webber, Doug Christie, Bobby Jackson, Mike Bibby, and Peja Stojakovic. The city of Sacramento supported the team with a record 354 straight sellouts.

With five cities that have housed this franchise, the Kings are the most traveled organization in the history of the NBA. From east to west, the Kings' franchise has run the gamut of highs and lows and continues to thrill NBA fans with energetic play that started in Rochester.

601 Free throw percentage (.601) on 122 of 203 from the line by Olden Polynice during the 1996 season. Polynice reportedly made $2.5 million in salary that year.

602 Number of steals (602) taken by the 1986 Sacramento Kings. The Kings also added 288 blocks to their defensive records that season.

603 Coach Les Harrison's winning percentage (603) during the 1950-51 NBA season. His Rochester Royals posted a 41-27 record and ironically, despite it being the second worst performance by a team

under his lead in his seven year coaching career, won the franchise's sole championship that year.

604 Team leading career field goal percentage (.604) by a Kings franchise player, recorded by Steve Johnson. The former Oregon State University standout ended his career in 1991 after playing for seven different teams including the KC Kings, Chicago Bulls, SA Spurs, Portland Trailblazers, Minnesota Timberwolves, Seattle Supersonics, and the Golden State Warriors.

605 Free throw percentage (.605) posted by Scot Pollard during his last season with the Kings in 2003 on 40-87 from the line. Side note: Pollard has filled in as a color analyst with the Sacramento Kings and the WNBA's Monarchs. He also hosted *Planet Pollard* for the Boston Celtics on *Comcast* SportsNet.

606 Free throw percentage (.606) by Corliss Williamson during the month of February in 2006. That year, Corliss posted a .776 average from the line by knocking down 38 of his 49 free throw attempts.

607 League leading true shooting percentage (.607) by sharp shooter and four time NBA All-Star Johnny Green during his 1971 season with the Cincinnati Royals. NBA Hall of Famer Bob Cousy coached Green that year and together they finished third in the NBA Central Division.

608 Number of steals (608) collected by the Sacramento Kings during the 2006 season. The Kings also rejected 299 shots en route to a 44-38 regular season record, advancing to the postseason for the eighth consecutive year.

609 NBA league leading field goal percentage (.609) by Mikki Moore during the 2007 season. In 2008, Moore put up a very respectable .577 field goal percentage.

610 Winning percentage (.610) for the 2004-05 Sacramento Kings. The Kings finished the regular season at 50-32 and made the

playoffs for the seventh consecutive time before falling to the Seattle Supersonics in the first round of the playoffs, 4-1.

611 Winning percentage (.611) for the 1953-54 Rochester Royals. The Royals finished the regular season at 44-28 before falling to the Minneapolis Lakers 2-1 in the Western Division Finals.

612 The number of minutes (612) that Mike Bibby, Doug Christie, Peja Stojakovic, Chris Webber and Brad Miller were on the court at the same time during the 2004-05 season. The five-man roster scored 1,326 points and allowed 1,234 while on the court together.

613 Winning percentage (.613) for the Sacramento franchise vs. the Los Angeles Clippers through the 2008 season. After 168 meetings, the Kings hold a 103-65 edge in head-to-head meetings.

614 Winning percentage (.614) of Coach Rick Adelman during his career in the NBA through the 2008 season. Adelman has made coaching stops in Sacramento, Portland, Golden State, and Houston.

615 Winning percentage (.615) of the Sacramento Kings during November of 2006. The Kings compiled an 8-5 record that month while outscoring their opponents 1,289-1,254.

616 The number of three point attempts (616) jacked up by the Kings' opponents during the 1992 season. Sacramento launched 675 of their own and cashed in on 238 treys that year.

617 Career free throw percentage (.617) through the 2008 season for former Sacramento King Jerome James. James was drafted by the Kings in the second round of the 1998 NBA draft and played in Sacramento for one season before moving north to Seattle.

618 Winning percentage (.618) of the Sacramento Kings versus the New Jersey Nets through the 2008 season. The Kings and Nets have met up 68 times and the Kings command a 42-26 lead in head-to-head games.

619 Month and day (6/19) in 2007 that the Sacramento Kings hired Reggie Theus as their new head coach. Nine days later, the team selected 7'0" center Spencer Hawes as the tenth overall selection in the 2007 NBA draft.

620 Number of games (620) played by the Rochester Royals. Their overall record from 1949-57 was 357-263 for a .576 winning percentage.

621 Winning percentage (.621) for the 1951-52 Rochester Royals. The Royals finished the regular season at 41-25, winning another division title only to lose in the playoffs to the Minneapolis Lakers 3-1 in the Western Division Finals.

622 Number of career assists (622) tallied by former Sacramento King Joe Kleine during his 15 year stint in the NBA. Kleine played four and a half seasons in Sacramento and helped the Kings to one playoff appearance in 1985-86 where he averaged 15 minutes of playing time per contest.

623 The number of minutes (623) played by Otis Thorpe during the Kings' 1998 season. That year, Thorpe shared time with the Vancouver Grizzlies. For the season, Thorpe tallied 2,197 minutes of playing time.

624 The single season franchise record for field goal percentage (.624), held by Steve Johnson. During the 1982-83 season, just his second in the league, Johnson hit 271 of 595 shots taken and was better from the floor than the line, where he averaged .574 (186 of 324).

625 Field goal percentage (.625) on 5-8 shooting for Doug Christie vs. the Utah Jazz in Game 1 of their 2002 first round playoff series. Christie scored 17 points and dished out four assists, but it was the Kings' Chris Webber who led all Kings' scorers with 24 points as Sacramento won the contest 89-86.

626 Free throw percentage (.626) posted by Joe Meriweather during his 1983 season with the Kansas City Kings. Meriweather played ten seasons in the league and was an All-Rookie selection.

627 Month and day (6/27) in 2000 that the Sacramento Kings' Assistant Coach Byron Scott accepted the head coaching job with the New Jersey Nets. After leaving Sacramento, Scott took his Nets to two NBA Finals appearances. The 2008 NBA Coach of the Year is currently coaching the New Orleans Hornets.

628 Month and day (6/28) in 1855 that the Sigma Chi Fraternity was established at the University of Miami in Oxford, Ohio. Sacramento Kings owners Joe and Gavin Maloof are members of this fraternity.

629 Winning percentage (.629) recorded by the 1952-53 Rochester Royals after posting a 44-26 record. The Royals would go on to the Division Semifinals before losing to Fort Wayne, two games to one.

630 Month and day (6/30) in 1965 that King legend Mitch Richmond was born in Fort Lauderdale, Florida. The six-time NBA All-Star won his sole championship with the 2002 Los Angeles Lakers.

631 Number of steals (631) snagged by the Kings' defense during their 1991 season. The Kings were led by Lionel Simmons' 113 steals. Ironically, Simmons also led the team in turnovers with 230 flubs.

632 League leading field goal percentage (.632) by 1981 Kansas City Kings first round draft selection Steve Johnson during his 1986 season with the San Antonio Spurs. Johnson also led the NBA in fouls committed in 1982 (372) and 1987 (340).

ALL-STAR SBTN NUMBER

633 The career winning percentage (.633) of coach Rick Adelman. Adelman posted a 395-229 record over 624 games coached between 1999 and 2006 and is the most successful coach in the history of the franchise in terms of wins and winning percentage. Les Harrison is the only other coach in franchise

history to post a winning percentage above .600 with a .620 winning percentage over 476 games coached, but he does have one up on Adelman . . . he is the only franchise coach to win a NBA championship.

634 Winning percentage (.634) of the Sacramento Kings during home games in the 1996 season. The Kings posted a 26-15 record on their home court while only winning 13 games on the road that season.

635 Number of field goals (635) made by Mitch Richmond during his 1994 season with the Sacramento Kings. That year, the 28 year old led all King scorers and scored a total of 1,823 points.

636 Free throw percentage (.636) by 6'9" forward Brian Grant during his 1995 season with the Kings. Sacramento had ten players on the 1995 squad with a free throw percentage of over .600.

637 Effective shooting percentage (.637) for the Kings' combination playing unit of Mike Bibby, Cuttino Mobley, Peja Stojakovic, Darius Songaila, and Brad Miller during the 2004-05 NBA season.

638 Total number of rebounds (638) secured by Bill Robinzine during his 1979 season with the Kansas City Kings. Robinzine is seen on the highlight footage of Darryl Dawkins shattering a backboard at Kansas City's Municipal Auditorium. Robinzine can be seen running away from the flying glass with his face in his hands during the play to shield his eyes. Dawkins named the dunk, "Robinzine Cryin."

639 Number of points (639) scored by Arnie Johnson during his 1951 season with the World Champion Rochester Royals. Although Johnson only spent five seasons in the league, he did lead the NBA in true shooting percentage, twice.

640 The number of field goal attempts (640) launched by Billy Owens during the 1997 NBA campaign. Of those shot attempts, Owens drained 299 of them for a .467 percentage. Owens was the fifth leading scorer on the team that season.

641 Number of field goals (641) made by former University of Louisville star Francisco Garcia during his first three seasons in Sacramento. The 23rd overall selection in the 2005 NBA draft, Garcia was a silver medalist at the 2003 Pan American Games held in Santo Domingo for team Dominican Republic.

642 Free throw percentage (.642) of Steve Johnson during his 1982 season with the Kansas City Kings. Johnson played two full seasons for the Kings' organization before heading to Chicago during the 1983-84 season.

643 Number of points (643) scored by the Kansas City Kings during the month of April in 1976. March was the only month during the 1976 season that the Kings outscored their opponents. Fortunately for Kings' fans, they did outscore their opponents at home, 4,320-4,185.

644 Number of field goals (644) attempted by Steve Johnson during the Kings' 1982 season. That year, Johnson hit 395 of those shots en route to scoring 1,002 points. Johnson was the third leading scorer on the team that year.

645 Number of words (645) in the January 10, 2004 AP article "While Webber watches, Kings take NBA scoring lead." The article was written by Greg Beacham, an Associated Press writer, and highlighted Peja's play after Webber had knee surgery.

646 Number of points (646) scored by LaSalle Thompson during his last season with the Kings' organization. Thompson played six full seasons with the Kings after playing his college ball at the University of Texas. After three years with UT, Thompson was the fifth overall selection in the 1982 NBA draft by the Kansas City Kings.

647 Number of field goals (647) made by two time NBA and three time ABA All-Star Larry Kenon during his 1980 season with the San Antonio Spurs. Kenon holds the NBA record for most steals (11) in a single game. Unfortunately for Kings' fans, he recorded this feat on December 26, 1976 vs. the Kansas City Kings.

648 Number of game appearances (648) tallied by former UCLA star Michael Sanders during his 11 season NBA career. Sanders never suited up for the Kings, but was a fourth round Kansas City selection in the 1982 draft.

649 Three point shots (649) attempted by the 1990 Sacramento Kings. The team recorded a .333 average on 216 treys and was led by Danny Ainge's 108 downtown shots made.

650 The team payroll (65.0) in millions anticipated by the 2008-09 Kings. The team's payroll ranks them 12th in the NBA when it comes to spending, nowhere near to money spent by the Knicks, who spent almost $94 million. Before being traded to the Bulls, the Kings' highest paid player in 2008-09 was Brad Miller ($11.4 million), who earned less than half of league leader Kevin Garnett's $25 million.

651 Number of steals (651) credited to the 2008 Sacramento Kings squad. Of the 651 snags, Ron Artest is credited with a team high 133 thefts. Francisco Garcia recorded 96 of his own that year, respectively.

652 NBA league leading number of free throws (652) made by former Kansas City – Omaha King Nate Archibald during the 1974-75 season. The Hall of Famer led the league in free throws made on three separate occasions.

653 Free throw percentage (.653) posted by Chris Webber during the 2003 playoffs. Webber dropped 32 of his 49 attempts while scoring 166 points that postseason.

654 Number of field goal attempts (654) by Sacramento's Shareef Abdur-Rahim during his 2006-07 season with the Kings. The native of Marietta, Georgia was named Mr. Basketball in back-to-back seasons and led his high school to a state title in 1994.

655 Free throw percentage (.655) posted on 38 of 58 shooting by Spencer Hawes during his 2008 season with the Kings. The 7' center

and former University of Washington standout saw action in 71 games in 2008 while starting in eight contests.

656 Number of steals (656) surrendered by the Kings' offense during the 2006 NBA season. Mike Bibby and Brad Miller led the team in turnovers that year with a combined 379 give-aways.

657 Charity shot percentage (.657) recorded by Otis Thorpe during the Kings' 1998 season. The 6'9" Thorpe made it to the line 70 times and drained 46 of those attempts.

658 Winning percentage (.658) of former Sacramento Kings' Assistant Coach Pete Carril during his coaching days at Princeton. While in New Jersey, Carril compiled a 514-261 record and won 13 Ivy League championships. Carril coached the Kings for ten seasons until his retirement in 2006.

659 The number of points (659) scored by Corliss Williams during the strike shortened 1999 season. During his 50 games played, Corliss would become the team's third leading scorer.

660 The number of points (660) scored by Wayman Tisdale during the Kings' 1990-91 season. Tisdale would play in only 33 games for Sacramento that year, but would still be the team's fifth leading scorer.

661 Free throw percentage (.661) posted by former Sacramento King Jason Hart during the team's 2006 season. Hart, a former Syracuse standout, played one full season with the Kings and scored a total of 261 points for Sacramento.

662 Free throw percentage (.662) tallied by Don Henriksen during his 1955 season with the Rochester Royals. A former star at the University of California, Henriksen played two seasons in the league and averaged 7.2 points per game.

663 NBA league leading number of free throws (663) made by Tiny Archibald during his 1973 campaign. Those free throws made also helped Archibald lead the league in most points scored at 2,719.

664 Total number of rebounds (664) collected by Hall of Famer Jack Twyman during his 1960 season with the Cincinnati Royals. Twyman led the team in points scored that season with 2,338 points.

665 NBA league leading number of free throws (665) made by Oscar Robertson during the 1964-65 season with the Cincinnati Royals. That season, Robertson came in second in the NBA MVP balloting behind the Boston Celtics Bill Russell.

666 Fittingly, the number of steals (666) recorded by the Kings' opponents during the 2000-01 NBA season. Sacramento secured 793 thefts of their own that year.

667 Winning percentage (.667) vs. the now defunct Chicago Stags team. The Kings organization won 8 of their 12 meetings. The Stags played four seasons in the BAA/NBA from 1947-50 before closing up shop.

668 The number of field goals (668) made by Mitch Richmond during his 1995 season with the Kings. Richmond was the only Sacramento player that year to log over 3,000 minutes of play.

669 The number of steals (669) collected by the Sacramento Kings during their 1994 season. Lionel Simmons led the squad with 104 steals of his own. Mitch Richmond also had over 100 thefts, respectively.

670 Number of steals (670) snagged by the Kings' Mitch Richmond during his seven year stint in Sacramento. The Olympic gold and bronze medalist finished his career with 1,211 steals.

671 Winning percentage (.671) for the 2003-04 Sacramento Kings. The Kings finished the regular season at 55-27 and made the playoffs for the sixth consecutive time before losing to the Minnesota Timberwolves in the Western Conference Semi-Finals, 4-3.

672 Total number of rebounds (672) collected by Hall of Famer Jack Twyman during his 1961 season with the Cincinnati Royals. Twyman was the team's second leading scorer that year with 1,997 points.

673 Number of points (673) scored by Kevin Martin during his junior season at Western Carolina in 2004. That season he also dropped in 206 free throws for the Catamounts.

674 The number of steals (674) credited to the 2004-05 Sacramento Kings. The team was led by Mike Bibby's 124 snags. Bibby also collected 30 blocks on the year.

675 Total number of field goals (675) made by Oscar Robertson during his postseason career with the Cincinnati Royals and the Milwaukee Bucks. The "Big O" found the playoffs in ten different campaigns during his NBA career. During the postseason, Robertson averaged 22.2 points per game.

676 Free throw percentage (.676) compiled by Kenny Thomas during his 2006 season with the Kings. Thomas attempted 204 free throws that year and netted 138 of them. He finished the season with 748 points scored.

677 Seasonal team high number of free throws (677) made by Tiny Archibald during his 1971-72 season with the Cincinnati Royals. That year, Nate attempted a NBA seasonal record 824 shots from the charity stripe.

678 The number of minutes (678) played by the Kings' Rick Calloway during his 1991 season with the Kings. Calloway played one year of NBA ball after a standout career with Kansas. He was selected by the Omaha Racers of the Continental Basketball Association during their 1990 draft and also played pro ball in Argentina and Poland.

679 Free throw percentage (.679) by Bonzi Wells during his 2005-06 season with the Kings on 129-190 shooting from the charity

stripe. That same year, Wells was listed on *GQ* magazine's Ten Most Hated Athletes list.

680 Number of career games (680) played by former Sacramento King Greg Kite. Kite played one season in SAC during 1990 and scored 230 points for the Kings.

681 Number of total rebounds (681) secured by Brad Miller during his 2008 season with the Kings. This brings his career total to 5,014 boards through the 2008 season.

682 Minutes (682) played by Tony Delk during his 2000 season with the Kings. Before Delk made the leap to the pros, he was the team leader of the 1996 University of Kentucky NCAA national championship team.

683 Free throw percentage (.683) compiled by the Kings during the 1999 strike-shortened season. Sacramento tossed up 1,293 free shots and made 883 of them. Their opponents faired a bit better by posting a .712 average from the line.

684 Number of games (684) played by Bobby Jackson during his career through the 2007-08 season. He has started 133 of those contests.

685 Points per game average (68.5) posted by the 2005 Sacramento Monarchs. That season, the Monarchs finished the year with a 25-9 record and won the organization's lone WNBA title. Like the Kings, the team is owned by the Maloof family.

686 Number of field goal attempts (686) by Joe Kleine during his 1988 season with the Kings. Kleine hit 324 of those shots and finished the year with 801 points as the fourth leading scorer on the team.

687 Month and year (6/87) that legendary Hall of Famer Bill Russell took over as head coach of the Sacramento Kings. Unfortunately for Kings' fans, the magic he had in Boston as head coach (two world

titles), did not follow him to Sacramento. Russell would compile an overall record of 17-41 as leader of the Kings.

688 Winning percentage (.688) recorded by the 1963-64 Cincinnati Royals after posting a 55-25 record. The Royals would go on to the Division Finals before losing to Boston, four games to one.

689 Number of points (689) scored by the Utah Jazz vs. the Kansas City Kings during the 1982 season. During the teams' six game regular season series, the Kings scored 674 points of their own as the two teams split 3-3.

690 NBA league leading number of assists (690) dished out by Oscar Robertson during his 1960-61 rookie season with the Cincinnati Royals. During his career, Robertson led the league in lend-a-hands six times.

691 Career number of assists (691) recorded by Reggie King from 1980-85. King played four full seasons for Kansas City before being dealt to the Seattle Supersonics. King was the 18th overall selection in the 1979 NBA draft by the Kings.

692 Winning percentage (.692) logged by the Kansas City Kings in games decided by less than four points during their 1982-83 season. In games decided by more than 11 points, the Kings posted an 18-13 record.

693 The regular season winning percentage (.693) by the Kings during the six seasons that they won their division. The Rochester Royals set a franchise record for winning percentage of .750 during the 1948-49 season when they posted a 45-15 record. They matched it the following season when they posted a 51-17 record. Two years later, the Royals posted a 41-25 mark, for a winning percentage of .621. The 1978-79 Kansas City Kings won their division with a record of 48-34 and a winning percentage of .585. Finally, the 2001 and 2002 Kings won back-to-back division titles with a record of 61-21 (.744) and 59-23 (.720), respectively. Over the six division titles, the teams had a combined record of 305-135.

694 Free throw percentage (.694) by Otis Birdsong during his 1980 season with the Kings on 286 of 412 from the line. Birdsong led the team in scoring that year with 1,858 points.

695 Number of minutes (695) played by the Kings' Brian Skinner during his 2005 season with the Kings. Skinner was part of the Philadelphia 76ers – Sacramento trade that sent Chris Webber to Philly.

696 Free throw percentage (.696) of Gil McGregor during his rookie season with the 1972 Cincinnati Royals. Although *Sports Illustrated* listed McGregor as the possible "rookie sleeper of the year," the former Wake Forest standout only played in the NBA for one season and never made it to a sophomore year.

697 Free throw percentage (.697) on 101 of 145 shooting by Billy Owens during the Kings' 1997 season. Owens ended the year as the Kings' fourth leading scorer by dropping 724 points.

698 Number of points (698) scored by Sacramento's Mikki Moore during his 2007-08 season with the Kings. Moore pumped in 282 field goals on 489 attempts. His 698 points were sixth best on the team in 2008.

699 The number of steals (699) tallied by the Kings' opponents during the 1991 season. That year, Sacramento's defense recorded 631 of their own snakes and also blocked 513 shots.

700 Time (7:00) in the evening on Wednesday, November 5, 2008 that the Sacramento Kings hosted the Memphis Grizzlies in the Kings home opener for the 2008-09 season.

Mike Bibby

Sacramento Kings

"All that's in the past."

— Gavin Maloof, owner Sacramento Kings

Chapter Eight

The Departed

The list is long.

In building a championship team, one must do what isn't necessarily popular among the masses. If you look at a recent departure list of players who seemed to have the Kings going in the right direction, you may scratch your head and wonder why the franchise let certain players go and traded others.

But as Geoff Petrie, Kings Basketball President, explains, sometimes you must make moves. "You're looking at the total picture with your team going forward, and how much better can it get the way it is versus what is the potential to get better by doing something different. What we decided to do is do something different. You know, if you have a big shade tree, shade's good to a point. But if there's too much shade, then the grass doesn't get to grow."

For some fans, it is hard to understand this logic, but for the Kings, it wasn't a matter of reloading from the early 2000s, it was a rebuilding that needed to take place. And rebuild they did. Kevin Martin, Beno Udrih, and Francisco Garcia are ready and willing to go the distance and get the

Kings back into the postseason for the first time since 2006. Everyone involved knows that it may take time though and that is why the Kings have faith in newcomers Jason Thompson, Donte Greene, and Spencer Hawes to deliver as well. The Kings are knocking on the door and the move to shift to younger players may be the key.

Below is a partial list of players who left the Kings and went on to play with other NBA teams—for better or worse:

Mike Bibby, 1999 NBA All-Rookie selection
Ron Artest, 2004 NBA All-Star and Defensive Player of the Year
Chris Webber, Five time NBA All-Star and 1994 Rookie of the Year
Peja Stojakovic, Three time NBA All-Star and 2004 All-NBA selection
Vlade Divac, 2001 NBA All-Star
Doug Christie, Four time NBA All-Defensive selection
Scot Pollard, 2008 NBA world champion
Hedo Turkoglu, 2008 NBA Most Improved Player

And then there is Bobby Jackson, 2003 Sixth Man of the Year. Welcome back. The Kings felt a need to have a veteran directing the young cast of characters during this rebuilding process and felt Jackson was the right man for the job. He returns to the Kings' lineup for the 2008-09 season. "I'm happy to be back," Jackson said. "Trust me; we'll work very hard out there."

Kings fans know you will.

701 Free throw percentage (.701) by Mikki Moore during his home games in 2007. Moore shot better away from Sacramento and posted a .768 charity stripe average on the road.

702 Free throw percentage (.702) by Lionel Simmons on 59 of 84 shooting from the line during the 1995 season. Remarkably, this was his lowest free throw percentage output during his NBA career.

703 Free throw percentage (.703) tallied by Chris Webber on 324 of 461 from the stripe during the 2001 season. Webber recorded six seasons above .700 during his NBA career.

704 Free throw percentage (.704) of Sacramento King Lorenzen Wright during games played with one day rest in 2000. Wright shot better that year with two days' rest; recording a .750 average.

705 Month and year (7/05) that Strength and Conditioning Coach Al Biancani retired from the Sacramento Kings. Biancani spent 18 years with the team. He received his Doctorate in Physical Education/Sociology from Utah State in 1972 and has been directing a fitness and physical therapy business for over 23 years in the Sacramento area.

706 The winning percentage (.706) of the Rochester Royals in their inaugural season of the National Basketball League. With a roster that would include names like NFL great Otto Graham, MLB catcher Del Rice, and MLB infielder and actor Chuck Connors, the Royals posted a 24-10 record during the regular season. The team would shock the Fort Wayne Zollner Pistons and sweep the Sheboygan Red Skins in the playoffs to claim the 1945-46 NBL title. Three years later the team would join the NBA, and 27 years later the team, after moves to Cincinnati and Kansas City, would settle down in Sacramento.

707 Field goal attempts (707) by Beno Udrih during his 2007-08 season with the Kings. Beno started 51 games for Sacramento that year and ended the season with 138 points scored.

708 Month and year (7/08) that the Sacramento Kings signed both Beno Udrih and Jason Thompson to multi-year contracts. Udrih signed a five year contract while the Kings worked out a deal with Thompson, the 12th overall pick in the 2008 draft.

709 Attendance of paid fans in the thousands (709) who attended Kings' games at ARCO Arena during the 2007 season. This was 16th best in the NBA that year out of a possible 30.

710 Month and day (7/10) in 2008 that the Kings' Brad Miller was suspended by the NBA for five games beginning at the onset of the 2008-09 season for violating the league's substance abuse policy.

711 Free throw percentage (.711) posted by the 1995 Sacramento Kings. That season, Spud Webb led the squad with a .934 average from the charity stripe as seven players averaged over .700 from the free throw line.

712 Free throw percentage (.712) compiled by the 1958 Cincinnati Royals. That year, Hall of Famer Clyde Lovellette recorded a .743 average from the line and led the NBA in the number of field goals made with 679 buckets.

713 Charity stripe percentage (.713) recorded by Vlade Divac during the Kings' 2003 season. Divac connected on 179 of his 251 attempts that year and ended the season with 795 points.

714 Free throw percentage (.714) tallied on five of seven shooting from the charity stripe by Sacramento's Lionel Simmons during his 1996 playoff series vs. the Seattle Supersonics. The Kings sneaked into the postseason after posting a 39-43 regular season record and finishing fifth in the Pacific Division.

715 Number of minutes (715) played by Matt Barnes during his 2005 season in Sacramento. Through the 2008 season, the UCLA product has played for the Clippers, Kings, Knicks, Sixers, and Warriors.

716 Number of points (716) scored by Connie Dierking during his 1967 season with the Cincinnati Royals. The former University of Cincinnati standout played five full seasons for the Kings' organization.

717 The number of field goal attempts (717) jacked up by Peja Stojakovic during the 2000 NBA season. That year, Peja tossed in 877 points as the Kings fourth leading scorer.

718 Free throw percentage (.718) logged by Greg Hyder during his lone season in the NBA. Hyder was drafted out of Eastern New

Mexico University as a Cincinnati Royals' third round selection in the 1970 NBA draft.

719 Free throw percentage (.719) of Michael Jackson during his 1988 season with the Kings on 23 of 32 shooting from the line. Before playing three seasons with the Kings, Jackson was a member of Georgetown's 1984 NCAA national championship team.

720 Winning percentage (.720) of the 2003 Sacramento Kings after posting a 59-23 regular season record. The team finished first in the Pacific Division, but was ousted by the Utah Jazz in the Western Conference semis. That year's attendance at ARCO was 709,997 which ranked 12th in overall NBA attendance.

721 Free throw percentage (.721) recorded by LaSalle Thompson during his 1985 season with the Kings. Thompson connected on 227 of his 315 charity shot attempts that year and finished the season with 965 points.

722 The number of steals (722) snagged by the Kings' opponents during the 1977 NBA season. The Kings recorded 849 thefts of their own that year. The Kansas City defense also posted 386 rejections to the season stats.

723 Free throw percentage (.723) of the 1997 Sacramento Kings on 1,494 of 2,067 shots from the free throw line. Four Kings' players drained over a .800 average that year from the charity stripe.

724 Number of points (724) scored by Billy Owens during his first full season with the Sacramento Kings in 1997. Owens was the third overall selection of the 1991 NBA draft after a stellar college career at Syracuse. In 1992 he was named to the first team All-Rookie club based on the 1,141 points, 639 rebounds, and 65 blocks he posted with the Golden State Warriors.

725 Month and day (7/25) in 1977 that the Kings' Kenny Thomas was born in Atlanta. "K-9" hosted "Thomas Toy Drive" in 2003

to help raise donations for Toys for Tots. It is typical to see him distributing food baskets at the Salvation Army, as well.

726 Number of field goals (726) made by former University of Oklahoma All-American Wayman Tisdale during his first full season with the Kings in 1990. Tisdale is also a jazz bass guitarist. He released his debut CD, *Power Forward* in 1995.

727 The number of steals (727) taken by the Kings' defense during their 1992 NBA campaign. The team also recorded 618 blocks that year.

728 Career free throw percentage (.728) posted by Don "The Kangaroo" Smith during his ten seasons in the NBA. Smith was selected by the Cincinnati Royals in the 1968 draft and played one season with the club. He has converted to Islam and goes by the name of Zaid Abdul-Aziz.

729 Free throw percentage (.729) recorded by the 1949-50 Rochester Royals. The team shot 1,690-2,319 from the charity stripe en route to a 51-17 record and a tie for the Central Division title.

730 Number of defensive rebounds (730) pulled down by the Kings' Kevin Martin from 2005-08. The former West Carolina University star was Sacramento's 26th overall selection in the 2004 NBA draft. Before leaving Western Carolina, Martin managed to score 1,838 points, which ranks fourth on the school's all-time list.

731 Month and day (7/31) in 2008 that the Kings NBA D-Affiliate announced its team name would be the Bighorns. The developmental team began its play in 2008 and is based in Reno, Nevada.

732 Free throw percentage (.732) recorded by the Kings' Corliss Williamson during home games played in 2003. He didn't sway at all on the road where he posted a .730 average.

733 Career playoff free throw percentage (.733) posted by Ron Artest through the 2007-08 season. Artest led the Kings to the postseason in 2006 where he dropped in 16 of 23 free tosses.

734 Career number of field goals (734) made by the Kings' Beno Udrih through the 2008 season. Udrih has two championship rings with the 2005 and 2007 San Antonio Spurs.

735 Number of steals (735) snagged by the 2003 Sacramento Kings. The team was led by Doug Christie's 180 thefts and followed by Chris Webber's 106 steals.

736 Number of points (736) scored by Bobby Wanzer during his 1951 season with the World Champion Rochester Royals. That season, the 6' guard posted a .401 average from the field on 252 of 628 shooting from the hardwood.

737 Free throw percentage (.737) on 84 of 114 shooting from the line by Vernon Maxwell during his 1999 season in Sacramento. Known more for his three point marksmanship, Maxwell led the NBA with 162 three point field goals made in 1992.

738 Career free throw percentage (.738) posted by former Sacramento King Sam Lacey during his 13 seasons of play. Lacey played 11 full seasons with the Kings' organization.

739 Free throw percentage (.739) posted by the Kings' Bobby Jackson during his 2001 season in Sacramento on 65 of 88 from the line. Jackson ended the season as the Kings' sixth leading scorer with 566 points scored.

740 Winning percentage (.740) for the Sacramento Kings organization versus the Memphis Grizzlies through the 2008 season. After 50 meetings, the Kings hold a 37-13 lead in head-to-head meetings.

741 Total number of steals (741) collected by the Sacramento Kings during their 2001-02 sprint to the Western Conference Finals.

During the season, the Kings only allowed their opponents to record 633 of their own.

742 Seasonal team high number of free throws (742) made by Oscar Robertson during his 1965-66 season with Cincinnati. That season, Robertson attempted 881 shots from the charity stripe.

743 Number of rebounds (743) pulled down by NBA All-Star Brad Miller during his 2004 season with the Sacramento Kings. A former standout at Purdue University, Miller averaged 5.3 points per game for Team USA at the 2006 World Championships in Japan.

744 Winning percentage (.744) of the 2002 Sacramento Kings after posting a 61-21 regular season record. The team finished first in the Pacific Division, but was ousted by the Los Angeles Lakers in the Western Conference Finals. That year's attendance at ARCO was 709,997 which ranked 15th in overall NBA attendance.

745 Number of field goal attempts (745) recorded by Corliss Williamson during the 1996-97 season. Williamson dropped in 371 of those shots and scored 915 points on the year. Not a perimeter player, Corliss took three treys and netted zero.

746 The number of minutes (746) played by Randy Allen during the Kings' 1989-90 season. Allen, a former standout at Florida State, played two seasons in Sacramento and scored a total of 252 points.

747 Auburn University single-season record for most points (747) scored by Sacramento Kings Assistant Coach Chuck Person during his 1985 season with the Tigers. In 1987 Person earned NBA Rookie of the Year honors with the Indiana Pacers.

748 Career NBA free throw percentage (.748) posted by Louie Dampier during his three seasons in the league. Dampier was also a seven time ABA All-Star with the Kentucky Colonels and was a fourth round Cincinnati Royals draft pick in the 1967 NBA draft.

749 Free throw percentage (.749) posted by the Sacramento Kings' opponents during the 2001 season. The Kings put their opponents on the line 1,724 times and were whistled for 1,596 fouls on the year.

750 Winning percentage (.750) for the 1949 and 1950 Rochester Royals. Rochester finished the 1949 season with a 45-15 record, winning the regular season Western Division only to fall in the playoffs to the Lakers. The next year, the Royals also finished first in their division only to get bumped out by the Pistons in the first round of the postseason.

751 Free throw percentage (.751) tallied by the Sacramento Kings during their 2001-02 sprint to a Pacific Division title. During the season, the Kings hit 1,618 free throws from the charity line.

752 Charity stripe percentage (.752) posted by Jason Williams during his 1999 season in Sacramento. The Pistol-Pete-like Williams made his way to the line 105 times and drained 79 for the year.

753 Free throw percentage (.753) on 1,692 of 2,248 shooting from the charity stripe by the 1951 World Champion Rochester Royals. Bobby Wanzer led the charge from the line by converting .850 of his free throws on 232 of 273 attempts.

754 Career free throw percentage (.754) posted by former University of Minnesota star Ron Behagen during his seven year stint in the NBA. Behagen played two seasons with the Kansas City – Omaha club and one more with the Kansas City Kings. Behagen may forever be known as a participant in the January 25, 1972 brawl between his Minnesota team and Ohio State. During the game, Behagen came off the bench and knocked Luke Witte unconscious. Ohio State coach Fred Taylor said it was, "the sorriest thing (he) ever saw in intercollegiate athletics." Behagen was suspended for the rest of the season.

755 Free throw percentage (.755) for Otis Thorpe during his 1988 season with the Kings. Thorpe tossed in 460 charity shots that year and became the team's leading scorer. He also led the club in total rebounds with 837 boards.

756 Charity shot percentage (.756) by Maurice Evans during his lone season in Sacramento in 2005. Evans, a former Longhorn at the University of Texas, has played four seasons with five different clubs through the 2008 season.

757 Number of field goal attempts (757) tallied by Derek Smith during his 1987 season with the Sacramento Kings. Smith, a former Louisville standout, scored 863 points that year as the Kings' fifth leading scorer.

758 The number of free throw attempts (758) and the number of assists (758) recorded by Hall of Famer Oscar Robertson during his 1963 season with the Cincinnati Royals. That season, Robertson was selected to the NBA All-Star team and to the first team All-NBA squad.

759 The number of steals (759) tallied and free throw percentage (.759) recorded by the Kings' opponents during the 1989 season. The Kings snagged 624 of their own steals and posted a higher free throw percentage at .770 in 1989.

760 Number of minutes (760) played by a thriller of a guard, Michael Jackson during his 1988 season with the Kings. Jackson found playing time in 58 contests that year and dished out 179 lend-a-hands.

761 Free throw percentage (.761) by Mikki Moore during home contests in 2004. Moore faired better on the road as he recorded a .815 average. As a starter that year, Moore posted a .944 average.

762 The number of minutes (762) played by Bob Bigelow during his four season NBA career from 1976 through 1979. Bigelow played two full seasons with Kansas City and was a first round selection by the Kings in the 1975 NBA draft.

763 Free throw percentage (.763) of former 1992 NCAA basketball tournament Most Outstanding Player Bobby Hurley on 58 of 76 shooting from the line during the 1995 Kings' season.

764 Number of points (764) scored by Jack Coleman during his 1951 season with the World Champion Rochester Royals. That season, the 6'7" forward/center dropped in 315 field goals and 134 free throws. Four years later, Coleman would make his only NBA All-Star appearance.

765 Number of points (765) collected by Cuttino Mobley during his 2005 season with the Sacramento Kings. Mobley may be best known for leading his University of Rhode Island squad to the NCAA Elite Eight in 1998.

766 Number of field goal attempts (766) recorded by Hall of Famer Nate Archibald during his 1981 season with the Boston Celtics. The former Royal/King reached a career high field goal attempts personal best with 2,106 shots in 1973.

767 Free throw percentage (.767) of the 1976 Kansas City Kings on 1,792 of 2,335 charity shots. The Kings were led from the line by Tiny Archibald's 501 free throws made.

768 The number of thefts (768) committed by the Sacramento Kings during their 1993 NBA season. The Kings made one more steal than their opponents that year and were led by Randy Brown's 108 snags.

769 Field goal percentage (.769) for Sacramento's Mitch Richmond during the 1994-95 NBA All-Star game. After scoring 23 points, grabbing four rebounds, and dishing out two lend-a-hands in 22 minutes on the court, Richmond took home NBA All-Star MVP honors.

770 Rebounds per game (7.70) grabbed by Pervis Ellison during his sophomore season in the league with the Washington Bullets. Before moving to Washington, Pervis played his rookie season in Sacramento where he collected 196 boards in 34 games played.

771 Winning percentage (.771) for the LA Lakers vs. the Kansas City Kings in 48 games played. The Cincinnati Royals faired best among Kings' franchise clubs against a Lakers team by winning .431 of their head-to-head contests.

772 Free throw percentage (.772) recorded by the 1988 Sacramento Kings on 1,795 of 2,324 shooting from the line. Otis Thorpe led the team with 460 charity shots made.

773 Charity stripe percentage (.773) posted by the 1952 Rochester Royals' club on 1,661 of 2,150 shooting from the free throw line. Bobby Wanzer led the team with a .904 average from the line.

774 Number of rebounds (774) brought down by Jack Coleman during his 1953 season with the Rochester Royals. Coleman played for two championship teams: the 1951 Royals and the 1957 St. Louis Hawks.

775 Number of three pointers (775) made that Mike Bibby drained while wearing a Kings' uniform. The 775 treys ranks third in franchise history.

776 Free throw percentage (.776) tallied by Larry Drew during his 1984 season in Kansas City. Drew played ten seasons in the league and is currently an assistant coach for the Atlanta Hawks team.

777 Total number of rebounds (777) collected by Chris Webber during the 2001 season. That year, Webber earned First-Team All-NBA honors.

778 Free throw percentage (.778) of former Kansas City – Omaha guard Mike D'Antoni during the 1975 NBA season. D'Antoni also holds a 267-172 NBA coaching record and has a .510 playoff winning percentage in 51 contests through the 2008 season.

779 Free throw percentage (.779) by #32 Francisco Garcia during his 2008 season. Garcia's game highs the season were 31 points, 12 rebounds, seven assists, five steals, and three blocks.

780 Charity stripe average (.780) by Mike Woodson during his 1981-82 season with the Kings. Woodson led the team in scoring that year with 1,221 points scored. He was second on the team in points per game with a 16.1 average.

781 Number of field goals (781) made by four time NBA All-Star Otis Birdsong during his 1980 season with the Kansas City Kings. Birdsong, the second overall pick in the 1977 draft out of the University of Houston, finished his NBA career with 12,544 points and a career shooting percentage of .506. In 2000, Birdsong was selected to the University of Houston's Hall of Honor.

782 Free throw percentage (.782) of Tyus Edney during his rookie season with the 1996 Sacramento Kings on 197 of 252 shooting from the line. Edney finished his NBA career with a .806 average.

783 NBA league leading number of free throw attempts (783) tossed up by Hall of Famer Nate Archibald during his 1973 season with Kansas City – Omaha. This was also Archibald's first season to make the All-Star roster.

784 Winning percentage (.784) vs. the Baltimore Bullets franchise. The Kings dominated the Bullets over time by tallying a 29-8 record and scoring 3,309 points to the Bullets 3,009.

785 Free throw percentage (.785) tallied by the 1977-78 season Kansas City Kings. The Kings dropped in 1,775 free throws that year and averaged 109.5 points per game.

786 Number of field goals (786) tossed in by Chris Webber during his 2000-01 season with the Sacramento Kings. Through the 2008 season, this ranks tenth on the Kings' all-time list for most field goals made in a single season.

787 Number of steals (787) snagged by the Kings during the 2000 season. Chris Webber led all Sacramento players with 120 thefts and Jason Williams tallied 117 steals, respectively.

788 The number of three point shots (788) attempted by the Sacramento Kings during their 1993 NBA season. The Kings converted on 262 of those attempts and were led by Walt Williams' 61 treys made.

789 Field goal shooting percentage (.789) vs. Golden State on March 18, 2008. This was the best shooting percentage by the Kings in a game-quarter that season.

790 Number of turnovers (790) forced by the Sacramento Kings' defense during the 1998-99 season. That year, the Kings recorded 444 steals and 232 blocks.

791 Month and year (7/91) that the Kings acquired 5'7" guard Spud Webb. That season the former dunk champion averaged 16 ppg for the Kings.

792 Free throw percentage (.792) recorded by Harold Pressley during his 1987-88 season with the Sacramento Kings on 103 of 130 shooting from the line. That season, Pressley dropped in 775 points.

793 Number of thefts (793) reported by King opponents during the 2001 NBA season. The Kings were led by the quick hands of Doug Christie and his 183 steals.

794 Career charity stripe percentage (.794) recorded by former Sacramento King Joe Kleine during his 965 game stretch in the NBA. Kleine posted 4,666 points while playing for seven NBA clubs.

795 Team leading number of rebounds (795) collected by Arnie Risen during his 1951 season with the Rochester Royals. The team tallied just over 3,000 boards on the year during their NBA championship season.

796 Free throw percentage (.796) logged in by the 1987 Sacramento Kings on 1,974 of 2,479 shooting from the line. Reggie Theus led the team with 429 charity shots made.

797 Total number of offensive rebounds (797) snagged by Doug Christie during his NBA career. Christie played for Sacramento from 2001-05 and made career stops with both LA clubs, the New York Knicks, Toronto, Orlando, and Dallas as well.

798 Points per game average (79.8) tallied by the 1953-54 Rochester Royals. The team finished the season with a 44-28 record and a second place position in the Western Division.

799 Field goal attempts (799) by Sacramento's John Salmons during his 2007-08 season with the Kings. The number 26 pick in the 2002 NBA draft scored 1,015 points in 2008 while dropping in 381 of his shots.

800 NBA league leading number of free throws (800) made by Oscar Robertson during the 1963-64 season with the Cincinnati Royals. That season, Robertson took home the hardware for NBA MVP and All-Star MVP.

Sacramento Kings
vs.
the Los Angeles Lakers

2001-02 Western Conference Finals

A statistical look at Game 6:

	Lakers	**Kings**
Final score	106	102
Free throws	34-40	18-25
4th-quarter FTs	21-27	7-9
Fouled out	None	Divac, Pollard
Fouls called	24	31
4th-quarter fouls	8	16

Officials: Dick Bavetta, Ted Bernhardt, Bob Delaney

"I have never seen officiating in a game of consequence as bad as that in Game 6."

—Michael Wilbon, The Washington Post

Chapter Nine

The Fix?

The best chance for the Kings' organization to win an NBA title since the Rochester Royals did in 1951 was the 2001-02 Sacramento Kings. Led by Chris Webber, the Kings reached the Western Conference Finals, only to lose to the LA Lakers in seven games.

After five games, Sacramento held a commanding 3-2 lead with a trip to Hollywood slated for May 31. The Kings had just won a 92-91 thriller at home and seemed destined for a trip to the NBA Finals vs. the New Jersey Nets. The Kings' franchise assumed only one thing stood in their way; the duo of Shaquille O'Neal and Kobe Bryant. What they neglected to account for was the officiating that is today rumored to have thrown Game Six and the series.

What is difficult to argue is the fact that the Kings had eight more personal fouls called on them in the fourth quarter, the Lakers shot 18 more free throws in the fourth, and two of the Kings' big men fouled out. These statistics don't lie.

When coupled with the testimony of a former NBA referee that suggests that two of the three refs working the game were "company men" and used "manipulation" to extend the series, it's hard to disregard these allegations. Allegedly, the NBA wanted to extend the series for television ratings and sponsorships; a claim that NBA Commissioner David Stern adamantly denies.

Some former Kings aren't so sure. "My first thought was: I knew it," Scot Pollard said. "I'm not going to say there was a conspiracy. I just think something wasn't right. It was unfair. We didn't have a chance to win that game."

Others disagree. NBA champion Bill Walton broadcast that game and believes there was no conspiracy by the NBA to throw the game or the series. "You're talking about some of the best referees ever in (Bob) Delaney and (Dick) Bavetta. I have never questioned their integrity."

More ammo for Kings fans to believe the worst: A team with players like Chris Webber, Peja Stojakovic, Mike Bibby, Doug Christie, Vlade Divac, Bobby Jackson, Scot Pollard, Lawrence Funderburke, and Hedo Turkoglu should not lose. This was a well assembled team with only one purpose: to win a world title.

Game Six ended with the Lakers on top 106-102, pushing the series to Game Seven in Sacramento. The Kings had their chances but dropped the final game 112-106 in overtime. Although the Kings claimed their first ever Pacific Division title, set franchise records for most wins, home victories, and road wins, they fell short of their ultimate goal.

If these allegations are true, the Kings' 61-21 regular season record was a waste and a shame. The group of players assembled by Sacramento never got a chance to raise the trophy and wear the ring. This may have been the Kings best chance at winning a title, but it won't be their last.

801 Number of points (801) scored by Joe Kleine during his 1987-88 season with the Kings. That year, Kleine popped in 324 shots, 153 free throws, and averaged 9.8 points per game.

802 Field goal attempts (802) recorded by Arnie Risen during the Rochester Royals 1952-53 season. That year, Risen popped in 295 of those shots and posted a 13.0 points per game average as the third leading scorer on the team.

803 Free throw percentage (.803) posted by Hall of Famer Oscar Robertson during his 1961-62 season with the Cincinnati Royals. Robertson went to the line 872 times that year and dropped in 700 of those attempts.

804 Number of rebounds (804) secured by Bob Boozer during the Cincinnati Royals' 1962 season. Only Wayne Embry and Oscar Robertson recorded more boards that year.

805 Free throw percentage (.805) on 107 of 133 shooting from the line by Billy McKinney during his 1979-80 season with the Kansas City Kings. After his stint in the NBA, McKinney became Assistant Vice President of Basketball Operations for the Chicago Bulls and Executive Vice President of the Seattle Supersonics.

806 Seasonal team high number of defensive rebounds (806) pulled down by Sam Lacey during his 1975-76 season with the Kansas City Kings. That year, Lacey recorded 1,024 total rebounds.

807 Free throw percentage (.807) tallied by Brad Lohaus during his 1989 season with the Sacramento Kings. Before making the leap to the pros, Lohaus was a McDonald's High School All-American. He then went on to play at the University of Iowa, helping the team to a NCAA Elite Eight appearance and a school record 30 win season.

808 Free throw percentage (.808) for former Sacramento King Wayman Tisdale during his last season with the Kings in 1994. Always a fighter, Tisdale underwent surgery in March of 2007 for cancer in his knee. Although he expected a 100% recovery, the 1984 Olympic gold medalist had to have a portion of his leg removed in August of 2008 to ensure the cancer would not spread.

809 Total number of rebounds (809) secured by Olden Polynice during his 1994 NBA season. That year, Olden played 31 games for the Kings and recorded 353 boards for Sacramento. He split the season between Sacramento and Detroit.

810 Number of points (810) scored by the Sacramento Kings' Hedo Turkoglu during his 2001-02 NBA campaign. Hedo is currently coming off a 2007-08 NBA Most Improved Player season with the Orlando Magic.

811 Free throw percentage (.811) posted by Jack Twyman during the 1961-62 NBA season. That year, Twyman averaged 22.9 points per game as the second leading scorer on the club and clocked 2,991 minutes of playing time.

812 The combined number of three pointers (812) made by the Kings and their opponents during the 2002 NBA season. The Kings tallied 426 treys that year and were led by Peja Stojakovic's 129 three-balls.

813 Points per game (81.3) scored by the Rochester Royals versus the Indianapolis Olympians from 1949-53. In 30 head-to-head matchups, the Royals beat the Olympians 18 times and outscored them by 115 points during those games.

814 Free throw percentage (.814) logged by Jerry Lucas during his 1965 NBA campaign. Lucas drained 298 charity shots and averaged 21.4 points per game as the Royals' second leading scorer.

815 Free throw percentage (.815) recorded by Mike Bibby during his 2004 season with the Kings. Bibby was the second leading scorer on the squad that year after dropping 1,506 points behind Peja Stojakovic's 1,964 points.

816 Career free throw percentage (.816) by former Sacramento King Jason Williams through the 2008 season. Williams played three full seasons with the Kings and drained 351 charity shots.

817 Number of minutes (817) played by Pete Chilcutt during his 1992 season with the Kings. The 6'10" forward was selected by Sacramento as the 27th overall pick in the 1991 NBA draft. Chilcutt played two full seasons with the Kings and ended his NBA career with 2,494 points scored.

818 Three point shooting percentage (.818) vs. Miami on March 2, 2008. This was the best trey percentage by the Kings in a game-half that season.

819 Free throw percentage (.819) logged by Kenny Smith during his 1987-88 season in Sacramento. The ten season NBA veteran concluded his career in 1997. That year he played for Detroit, Orlando, and Denver.

820 Number of games (820) played by the Kansas City Kings. Their overall record from 1976-85 was 381-439 for a .465 winning percentage.

821 Month and day (8/21) in 2008 that the Sacramento Kings held a Bobby Jackson press conference to announce the fan-favorite's return to the organization. In Jackson's words, "I'm happy to be back here. I'm in a great situation, coming back to a team and organization, and a community that I'm familiar with and happy to be back to."

822 Number of games (822) played by Big Nasty Corliss Williamson during his 12 season NBA career. The former Arkansas product started and ended his career in Sacramento with stops in Toronto, Detroit, and Philadelphia.

823 Free throw percentage (.823) by John Salmons during his 2008 season with the Kings. That year, Salmons drained 20 points in 18 of his games. He also snagged ten or more rebounds five times.

824 Winning percentage (.824) of the Portland Trailblazers vs. the Sacramento Kings in overtime games. This percentage is the third highest of one NBA team versus another in after regulation games. The teams' last matchup was a January 6, 2007 overtime thriller, which the

Blazers won 110-105, moving Portland's record against the Kings to 14-3 in overtime games.

825 Salary in the thousands of dollars (825) for Eddie House during his 2005 season with the Kings. House scored 237 points for Sacramento that year and compiled 550 minutes of play.

826 Career free throw percentage (.826) posted by Hall of Famer Tiny Archibald during five season appearances in the NBA postseason. Archibald helped the Kansas City – Omaha team to one playoff showing and scored 121 points during that playoff run in 1975.

827 Free throw percentage (.827) by former Head Coach Reggie Theus during his 1986 season with the Kings. Theus dropped in 405 charity shots that year and tallied 1,503 points. His 18.3 points per game was second behind Eddie Johnson's 18.7 ppg.

828 Charity shot percentage (.828) tallied by Brad Miller during his 2005-06 season with the Kings on 280 of 338 shooting from the line. Miller logged 2,923 minutes of play that year and ended the season with a 15 points per game average; fourth best on the team.

829 Number of offensive rebounds (829) pulled down by the 2008 Sacramento Kings. The Kings were out-boarded on the offensive end, as their opponents snagged 970 offensive rebounds of their own.

830 Charity shot percentage (.830) on 288 of 347 shooting from the line by Mike Bibby during his 2007 season with the Kings. Bibby played in all 82 games that year and logged 2,784 minutes of court time. Only Kevin Martin's 2,818 minutes played bettered Bibby's time.

831 Number of minutes (831) played by future Hall of Famer Chris Webber during his 2004 season with the Kings. Webber's chance at the Hall, according to www.basketball-reference.com, is over 69%.

832 Points per game (83.2) scored by the Rochester Royals versus the Washington Capitols during the teams' 16 meetings. During

those contests, the Royals outscored the Capitols 1,331 to 1,198 and checked the win column 13 times.

833 Winning percentage (.833) of the Sacramento Kings franchise vs. the now defunct Indianapolis Jets. The Jets participated in BAA play for one season as the Rochester Royals beat the Jets five of the six times they met during the 1948-49 campaign. That year, the Royals finished first in the Western Division while the Jets came in dead last with an 18-42 record.

834 Number of points (834) scored by Sacramento's Beno Udrih during his 2008 season with the Kings. The 2000 Slovenian League Rookie of the Year is averaging 7.1 points per game average through his first four seasons in the NBA.

835 Free throw percentage (.835) posted by Jim Les during the 1991 NBA season. Les popped in 86 charity shots that year and also drained 119 shots en route to a 7.2 points per game average.

836 Number of minutes (836) played by George Wilson during his 1969-70 season in the NBA. Wilson played two full seasons with the Cincinnati Royals and was selected by the franchise in 1964 as part of the league's territorial draft.

837 The number of points (837) scored by Happy Hairston during his 1967-68 season with the Cincinnati Royals. Happy dropped in 317 baskets and averaged 17.4 points per game that year.

838 Career playoff free throw percentage (.838) tallied by Sacramento King Mikki Moore through the 2008 season. Moore has visited the postseason party twice; once with Detroit and once with New Jersey, and is slated to again with Boston in 2009.

839 Number of points (839) scored by Quincy Douby during his 2005-06 season at Rutgers. The Sacramento King also drained a school record 116 treys during the same year.

840 The number of field goals (840) made during Oscar Robertson's 1964 season with the Cincinnati Royals. The 840 buckets ranked second that season in field goals made. The "Horse" never led the league in field goals made, but did finish as runner-up on three different occasions.

841 The total number of team leading rebounds (841) grabbed by Johnny Green during his 1970 season with the Cincinnati Royals. Green would finish his NBA career with just over 9,000 boards in 1,057 games played.

842 Number of turnovers (842) committed by the 1999 Sacramento Kings. Not only did Chris Webber lead the team in points scored that year, he also led the squad in turnovers with 148 giveaways.

843 Free throw attempts (843) by Hall of Famer Oscar Robertson during his 1967 season with the Cincinnati Royals. The "Big O" connected on 736 of those charity shots and ended the season with 2,412 points scored.

844 Playoff free throw percentage (.844) tallied by Jack Twyman during the Royals' 1963 season. During the team's 12 game playoff run, Twyman connected on 65 of his 77 charity shot attempts.

845 Number of assists (845) dished out by Oscar Robertson during his 1966-67 season with the Cincinnati Royals. As a team, the Royals recorded 1,858 lend-a-hands.

846 Points per game average (84.6) by the Rochester Royals during their 1951 NBA championship season. Arnie Risen led the team with 1,077 points as the Royals had six players score over 500 points.

847 Number of assists (847) dished out by Oscar Robertson during his 1965-66 season with the Cincinnati Royals. As a team, the Royals recorded 1,818 lend-a-hands.

848 Free throw percentage (.848) recorded by the Kings' Brad Miller during the 2007-08 season on 262 of 309 shooting from the line. Miller ended the year with 2,513 minutes played and 964 points scored.

849 Charity shot percentage (.849) tallied by Mike Bibby during his 2005-06 season with the Kings. Bibby drained 342 of his 403 attempts that year.

850 Team leading free throw percentage (.850) by Bobby Wanzer during his 1951 season with the Rochester Royals. That year, the Royals shot .753 from the line on 1,692 of 2,248 charity shots taken.

851 Charity shot percentage (.851) of Doug Christie on 206 of 242 shooting from the line during the 2001-02 season. Christie logged 2,798 minutes played and scored 972 points for the year.

852 Number of offensive rebounds (852) pulled in by the 2006 Sacramento Kings. Unfortunately, their opponents out-rebounded them on the offensive end of the court by pulling down 101 more boards than the Kings. Kenny Thomas led all Kings that season with 199 offensive boards of his own.

853 Free throw percentage (.853) recorded by Francisco Garcia during night games of the 2006 season. Garcia did much better at night, posting a .737 percentage during day games that year.

854 Playoff charity shot percentage (.854) posted by Doug Christie during the team's 2004 postseason push. That year, Christie hit 41 of his 48 free throw attempts and averaged 13.8 points per game during the Kings' 12 game playoff march.

855 Free throw percentage (.855) posted by Jim Jackson on 47 of 55 shooting from the line. Jackson averaged 7.7 ppg on the year, helping lead the Kings to the third best record in the NBA that year, 59-23.

856 Charity shot percentage (.856) tallied by Peja Stojakovic during his 2001 season with the Kings. That year, Peja drained 267 of his free throws and averaged 20.4 points per game.

857 Winning percentage (.857) of the Boston Celtics vs. the Sacramento Kings in overtime games. The Celts own a 12-2 career record against the Kings in after regulation games.

858 Free throw percentage (.858) recorded by Oscar Robertson during his 1964 postseason run with the Cincinnati Royals. Robertson drained 109 of his 127 charity shot attempts in ten games.

859 Charity stripe percentage (.859) recorded by Spud Webb during his 1992 season in Sacramento. Webb hit 262 of his 305 attempts that year and scored 1,231 points for the Kings; third highest on the team.

860 Total number of points (860) scored by Tyus Edney during his 1996 season with the Kings. During college, Edney scored 1,515 points in four seasons at UCLA.

861 Free throw percentage (.861) posted by future Hall of Famer Mitch Richmond during his 1997 season in Sacramento. As a team, the Kings shot a .723 average and drained 1,494 charity shots.

862 Points per game average (86.2) earned by the 1951-52 Western Division Champion Rochester Royals. The club was led that year by Bob Davies' 16.2 ppg average and by Arnie Risen's 841 total boards.

863 Number of steals (863) snagged by the Kansas City Kings during their 1979-80 season. Their opponents tallied 695 of their own.

864 Free throw percentage (.864) recorded by Mitch Richmond during his last season with the Kings in 1997-98. That year, Richmond dropped in 407 of his 471 attempts.

865 Career NBA free throw percentage (.865) tallied by Bob Arnzen during his one season in the league with the 1971 Cincinnati

Royals. Arnzen also played three seasons in the ABA where he posted a .652 free throw percentage.

866 Number of field goals (866) popped in by Oscar Robertson during his 1961-62 campaign with the Cincinnati Royals. Through the 2008 season, this ranks third on the Kings' all-time list for most field goals made in a single season. That year the "Horse" took home first team All-NBA honors.

867 Number of minutes (867) played during Clinton Wheeler's two season NBA career. Although Wheeler never played a minute for the Kings, he was drafted as the 150th overall selection in the 1981 NBA draft by the Kansas City Kings out of William Paterson University.

868 Kevin Martin's free throw percentage (.868) on zero days rest between games during his 2006 season. Martin shot best with no rest. With one day off, he shot .826, with two days off, he shot .857 from the line, and with three-plus days rest, Martin shot .840 from the charity stripe.

869 Kevin Martin's free throw percentage (.869) during the Kings' 2007-08 season on 502 of 578 shooting from the line. Martin dropped 1,443 points on his opponents that year and averaged 23.7 points per game.

870 Number of field goals (870) tossed in by Jack Twyman during his 1959-60 season with the Cincinnati Royals. Through the 2008 season, this ranks second on the Kings' all-time list for most field goals made in a single season.

871 Team leading free throw percentage (.871) earned by Vinny Del Negro during the Kings' 1990 season. Del Negro dropped in 135 of his 155 attempts that season and also scored 739 points on the year; fourth best on the club.

872 Total number of three point attempts (872) jacked up by Doug Christie during his four-plus seasons with the Sacramento Kings. Christie would go on to record 2,272 trey attempts during his career.

873 Number of points (873) scored vs. the Charlotte Bobcats through the 2008 season. The Kings hold an overall 5-3 record against the Bobcats while averaging 109.1 points per game.

874 Career free throw percentage (.874) by Kevin Martin during games played in November through the 2008 season. Martin's best monthly output is December. He drains .875 of his shots near the holidays.

875 Total number of field goals (875) made by former University of Florida star Jason Williams during his first three seasons in the NBA with the Kings. The playground baller picked up an NBA title as a member of Miami's 2006 squad.

876 Number of points (876) scored by Brad Miller during his 2004-05 season in Sacramento. In 56 games played, Miller ended the year with a 15.6 points per game average.

877 Free throw percentage (.877) on 64-73 shooting by the Kings' Jon Barry during the 2000-01 season. The former Georgia Tech star saw playing time with Milwaukee, Golden State, Atlanta, Sacramento, Detroit, Denver, Houston, and the Los Angeles Lakers.

878 Number of total rebounds (878) pulled in by Bob Boozer during his 1962-63 season with the Cincinnati Royals. The former Kansas State star and Omaha native was a member of the 1960 Olympic gold medal team that competed in Rome.

879 Free throw percentage (.879) by Brad Miller during games played in January of the 2007-08 season. Miller's best month during that season was November. He drained .918 of his free tosses.

880 Field goal attempts (880) jacked up by Bob Davies during his 1953 season with the Rochester Royals. Davies made 339 of those shots and ended his campaign with a 15.6 points per game average.

881 Number of minutes (881) played by Jim Les during his 1993 season with the Sacramento Kings. Les is currently the head coach at his

alma mater Bradley University. For the past three seasons, he has led the Braves to the NCAA, NIT, and College Basketball Invitational postseason tournaments.

882 Free throw percentage (.882) compiled by Peja Stojakovic during his 2000 season with the Kings. Peja had 153 attempts and sank 135 of them from the charity stripe.

883 Number of free throws (883) made on 1,293 shot attempts by the 1999 Sacramento Kings. That year, Vlade Divac led the charge with 255 charity stripe attempts. He made 179 of them.

884 Charity shot percentage (.884) recorded by Shareef Abdur-Rahim during games played vs. the LA Clippers in 1998. During those four games, Abdur-Rahim averaged 27.8 points per game.

885 Free throw percentage (.885) posted by Kevin Martin during March of the 2007-08 season. That month, he averaged 26.3 points per game and logged over 37 minutes of playing time per contest.

886 Number of minutes (886) played by Mike McGee during his 1988 season in Sacramento. The 28 year old McGee found the court in 37 games and scored 524 points on the year.

887 The prefix (887) of the Carl's Jr. restaurant phone number at 13312 Lincoln Way in Auburn, California that were offering Sacramento King bobbleheads in 2005 as part of a marketing promotion in conjunction with the Kings. The phone number to this particular Carl's Jr. is 530-887-9254.

888 Team leading career number of games (888) played in by a Kings franchise player, recorded by Sam Lacey from 1970-81. The former New Mexico State University standout was a 1975 NBA All-Star. During the same season, Lacey led the league in defensive rebound percentage at 28.3.

889 Free throw percentage (.889) posted by Mikki Moore during the 2007-08 season. Moore recorded six double-doubles that year and scored in double figures 31 times during the 2008 season.

890 Number of points (890) posted by Larry Drew during his 1986 season with the Kings. Side note: During ARCO Arena's first game on October 25, 1985, Drew shot 6 for 14, grabbed two boards, and scored 12 points. Drew was also NBA Player of the Month in December of 1982.

891 Number of points (891) scored when the 2004-05 Sacramento Kings drove to the paint. With penetration into the lane, the Kings tossed up 629 shot attempts.

892 Free throw percentage (.892) recorded by Ollie Johnson during the Kings' 1975 season in Kansas City. Johnson ended his NBA career with a .827 average by canning 868 of his 1,049 attempts.

893 Team leading career free throw percentage (.893) by a Kings franchise player, recorded by Peja Stojakovic during his seven-plus years with Sacramento.

894 Career free throw percentage (.894) for Peja Stojakovic through the 2007-08 season. This average ranks second among active NBA players through the 2008 season. Only former NBA MVP Steve Nash ranks higher with a .897 percentage.

895 The number of points (895) scored by Bobby Jackson during the 2002-03 season. Jackson would become the first and, thus far, only Kings player to win the NBA Sixth Man Award by averaging 15.2 points over 26 starts and 59 total games played for a squad that posted a 59-23 record and won the Pacific Division.

896 The number of points (896) scored by Bobby Jackson during the 2001-02 season. That season, Jackson would play in 81 games and average 11.1 points per game.

897 Free throw percentage (.897) for Doug Christie during his 2001 season in Sacramento. This percentage ranked third in the NBA

during the 2001 season behind Indiana's Reggie Miller and the Knicks' Allan Houston.

898 Minutes (898) played by Med Park during his 1959 season with the Cincinnati Royals. Park, a Missouri native, won a world title with the 1958 St. Louis Hawks.

899 Number of minutes (899) played by Derek Smith during the Kings' 1988 season in Sacramento. Side note: During the first game played in Sacramento, Smith shot 14 of 19 from the field and led all scorers with 36 points as a member of the LA Clippers on October 25, 1985.

900 Points per game average (90.0) scored by the Rochester Royals vs. the Providence Steam Rollers during the teams' five meetings. The Royals outscored their opponents 450-381.

Kevin Martin

Sacramento Kings

"He's (Kevin Martin) not just a big part of the present, but a large part of the future as well."

— Geoff Petrie, Kings President of Basketball Operations

Chapter Ten

The Future

Kings' fans must have been a little worried when Sacramento used a first round draft selection on a little known guard from Western Carolina University. Even with a 23.3 points per game average, Kevin Martin was not proving himself on a weekly basis like other guards from Kansas, Duke, and UCLA. Martin was playing in the Southern Conference and the conference did not have the same members as when it was chartered: Alabama, Kentucky, Maryland, North Carolina, and Virginia to name a few. No, Martin was going head to head with teams like Furman, Samford, and Wofford College.

The Maloof family must have seen something in the lanky kid from Zanesville, Ohio. Respectively, Martin was named All-District by the National Association of Basketball Coaches and by the United States Basketball Writers Association during his stint at Western. He was also a first team All-Southern Conference selection three years in a row. Still, not enough to convince true diehard Kings' fans that he was their savior.

That has changed.

The Kings' organization gave Martin a chance and he has repaid their kindness. Over the last four years, Martin has scored 3,970 points, dealt out 421 assists, grabbed 934 rebounds, and has fit into a leadership role while still managing to be a team player. He has everyone in Sacramento applauding, even former Head Coach Reggie Theus. "He's a bucking star who has everything together as a young man. You want your other younger players to emulate what Kevin is doing."

Although Martin has not been made an NBA All-Star yet, he is playing like one and it's only a matter of time before fans worldwide see what the Kings do. Geoff Petrie, President of Basketball Operations, is a believer as well, "He combines a lot of things that you like to see and want to see in a professional athlete. He's got talent, is motivated, willing to listen, and he's a terrific social conscious . . . "

Social is right. Martin takes his role in the community serious. He's made appearances at the Joe and Gavin Maloof youth basketball camps, hosted his own youth basketball clinics in Sacramento, raised money for paraplegic and quadriplegic patients, distributed food baskets at the Salvation Army, participated in a Reading Rally to benefit the Children's Aid Society, and helped refurbish and donate a Kings Reading and Learning Center in Sacramento.

And to honor Martin's commitment to the franchise and the city of Sacramento, the Kings signed him to a five year deal worth over $50 million and made him the face of the Kings and their future. Kings' fans can be guaranteed that Martin is worth the money. They can be guaranteed that the franchise made the right move in drafting him. They can be guaranteed that the playoffs will become common place in Sacramento. And, they can be guaranteed that Martin will be loyal.

Martin is the future.

901 Month and day (9/01) in 1975 that former Sacramento King Cuttino Mobley was born in Philadelphia, Pennsylvania. Mobley attended Maine Central Institute in Pittsfield before finding a place at the University of Rhode Island for his college ball. In 1998, Mobley was drafted in the second round of the NBA draft by the Houston Rockets.

902 Free throw percentage (.902) logged by Shareef Abdur-Rahim during his 2003 season with the Kings in games against the Indiana Pacers. During the teams' five game series, Shareef averaged 21 points per game.

903 Free throw percentage (.903) tallied by Adrian Smith during his 1967 season with the Royals. This percentage also led the league that year. Through the 2008 season, this ranks fifth on the Kings' all-time list for best free throw percentage posted in a single season. The former Kentucky standout earned one NBA All-Star nod in 1966.

904 Points (904) scored by Hall of Fame inductee Bob Davies during his 1949 rookie season with the Rochester Royals. That year, Davies would be named to the first team All-BAA squad after averaging 15.1 points per game.

905 Charity shot percentage (.905) tallied by Leon Wood on 19 of 21 shooting from the line during the 1990-91 season, his last in the NBA. A reserve, Wood played 12 games with the Kings and contributed to the cause by scoring 81 points.

906 Career number of games (906) played by former King Scott Wedman during his 13 seasons in the league. During those 906 games played, Wedman logged 25,927 minutes played.

907 Number of offensive rebounds (907) secured by the Kings' opponents during the 2006-07 NBA season. Sacramento recorded 797 of their own and were led by Kenny Thomas' 134 offensive boards.

908 The combined number of blocks (908) by the Sacramento Kings and their opponents during the 2001 NBA season. That year, the Kings rejected 432 shots en route to a 55-27 record.

909 The number of minutes (909) played by Walt Wesley during the Cincinnati Royals' 1966-67 season. That year, the Fort Myers, Florida native scored 314 points.

910 NBA league leading number of assists (910) by 1991 Hall of Fame inductee Nate Archibald, during the 1973 season. That year, the guard from the Bronx also led the league in minutes played (3,681) and field goals made (1.028).

911 Phone number (911) for the emergency services in Sacramento. The Associated Press reported on March 7, 2007 that Law Enforcement Deputies had responded to 911 calls from Ron Artest's home five times in less than a year, including two domestic disturbances.

912 Number of points (912) recorded by LaSalle Thompson during his 1987 season with the Kings. LaSalle was the first ever player to record a made free throw at ARCO Arena.

913 Number of minutes played (913) by Joe Kleine during the Kings' 1989 season and by Harold Pressley during the 1987 season. The two teammates combined for a career 21,514 minutes played.

914 Number of field goal attempts (914) jacked up by Kevin Martin during the 2007-08 season. Martin hit on 417 of those shots and averaged 23.7 points per game that year.

915 The number of points (915) scored by Travis Mays during the Kings' 1991 season. Mays was the Kings' second selection in the 1990 draft behind Lionel Simmons. Mays' first season in the league garnered second team All-NBA honors.

916 The area code (916) of the Sacramento Kings phone number. To reach the Kings' front office, dial 916-928-0000.

917 Winning percentage (.917) for the Rochester franchise vs. the now defunct St. Louis Bombers from 1948-1950. The Royals owned the Bombers, outscoring them 1,047 to 911. The Royals beat St. Louis 11 of the 12 times they met.

918 Number of minutes (918) logged by Walt Wesley during his 1968 season with the Cincinnati Royals. Wesley scored 452 points that year. The records show that Wesley made the top ten lists once in his

career. In 1971, Wesley ranked number nine in personal fouls committed with 295 hacks.

919 Month and day (9/19) in 1925 that former Rochester Royal Fran Curran was born. Curran, a former University of Notre Dame standout, played two seasons in Rochester and scored a total of 602 points.

920 Month and day (9/20) in 2008 that Kings' players Kevin Martin and Bobby Jackson put on a free basketball clinic in Oak Park. The clinic was open to 150 children.

921 League leading number of defensive rebounds (921) credited to Sam Lacey during his 1975 season with the KC-Omaha Kings. The NBA All-Star finished his career with 5,226 defensive boards.

922 Month and day (9/22) in 1993 that the Sacramento Kings hired Del Harris as a basketball consultant. Less than nine months later, Harris resigned. He would take over as head coach of the Los Angeles Lakers and win NBA Coach of the Year honors for the 1994-95 season.

923 Number of assists (923) handed out by former Sacramento King Brian Grant during his 12 season NBA career. Grant's best output in Sacramento was his 127 lend-a-hands posted in 1996.

924 Number of points (924) scored by the Rochester Royals' Jack Coleman during his 1955 All-Star season. This would be Coleman's only All-Star appearance as he scored six points in 19 minutes of playing time.

925 Number of points (925) scored by Bill Robinzine during his 1980 season with the Kansas City Kings. Robinzine, a DePaul product, was the Kings' first selection in the 1975 NBA draft.

926 The number of field goal attempts (926) posted by Arnie Risen during his 1952 season with the Rochester Royals. Risen scored 1,032 points that year for the Western Division champs.

927 NBA league leading free throw percentage (.927) tallied by three-time All-Star Peja Stojakovic during the 2003-04 season with the Kings. Peja, originally from Croatia, holds Greek citizenship and was a gold medalist for the Yugoslavian team at the 2002 FIBA World Championship games and the 2001 European Championships.

928 Month and day (9/28) in 1976 that former Sacramento King Bonzi Wells was born in Muncie, Indiana. Wells grew up in Muncie and attended Central High before attending Ball State University. Wells was a Pistons' first round pick in the 1998 NBA draft.

929 Month and day (9/29) in 1964 that former Sacramento King Brad Lohaus was born in New Ulm, Minnesota. Lohaus attended high school at Greenway High in Phoenix, Arizona before heading out to the University of Iowa. Lohaus played for the Kings in 1989.

930 The combined number of three pointers (930) made by the Sacramento Kings and their opponents during the 2000 NBA season. That year, the Kings drained 534 treys on 1,656 attempts for a .333 average.

931 Points per game average (93.1) compiled by the Kings during the 1997-98 season. Unfortunately, their opponents averaged 98.7 ppg of their own, as the Kings finished the season at 27-55. As a side note, Sacramento finished with a 21-20 record at home, extending their winning record at home to four straight seasons.

932 Number of minutes (932) played by former Sacramento King Brian Grant during his freshman season at Xavier. Grant finished his college career averaging 29.2 minutes played per game.

933 Free throw percentage (.933) recorded by Peja Stojakovic during his 2006 season in Sacramento. Peja hit 98 of his 105 attempts and scored 511 points before being dealt to the Indiana Pacers.

934 The franchise single season record for free throw percentage (.934), held by Anthony "Spud" Webb. The diminutive guard, who stood 5'6" and weighed just 133 lbs., made 226 free throws

out of 242 attempts in 76 games played over the course of the 1994-95 season. Spud would record over one-quarter of his total points on the season from the line.

935 Number of career wins (935) tallied by former Sacramento Head Coach Dick Motta. Motta posted a 935-1,017 record over a 25 year career that included one world title and a 1970 NBA Coach of the Year award.

936 Field goal attempts (936) by Bob Boozer during his 1961-62 season with the Cincinnati Royals. Boozer drained 410 of those shots and finished the year with a .438 shooting average.

937 During the 2006-07 season, Kings' opponents used the dunk shot on 5% of their attempts. Of those dunk attempts, opponents converted on (.937) percent of their shots. Kings' players only used the dunk 3% of the time and converted on .907 of their own shots.

938 Three point attempts (938) posted by former University of Oklahoma star Brent Price during his nine seasons in the NBA. Price concluded his career after his 2002 season with Sacramento. That year, Price played 20 games and scored 31 points.

939 Number of minutes (939) played by Don Buse during his 1985 season with the Kansas City Kings. The two time ABA All-Star led the NBA in three point field goals made in 1982 with 73 bombs.

940 Team leading number of field goals (940) attempted by Arnie Risen during the 1950-51 Rochester Royals season. Risen finished the year with 1,077 total points scored and a 16.3 points per game average.

941 Finishing place (9th) in ('41) for the Rochester Seagrams during the World Professional Basketball Tournament. The Seagrams were a predecessor to the Rochester Royals. That season, the tournament was won by the Detroit Eagles. The Seagrams were bested by the Kenosha team in the first round by a score of 40-36.

942 During the 2007-08 season, Kings' opponents used the dunk shot on 5% of their attempts. Of those dunk attempts, opponents converted on (.942) percent of their shots. Kings' players only used the dunk 4% of the time and converted on .948 of their own shots.

943 Number of three point attempts (943) jacked up by the 1999 Sacramento Kings. That year, the Kings hit 290 of those trey attempts for a .308 percentage. The team was led by Jason Williams' 100 three pointers made.

944 The number of minutes (944) played by Larry Staverman during his 1960-61 season with the Cincinnati Royals. Staverman played in Cincinnati for three seasons and was a ninth round pick in the 1958 NBA draft by the Royals.

945 Defensive rating (94.5) recorded by Sam Lacey during his 1973-74 season with the Kansas City – Omaha Kings. That year, Lacey compiled 126 steals and 184 blocks.

946 The number of minutes (946) played by Jawann Oldham during his 1988 season in Sacramento. The former Seattle University standout played a total of 5,241 minutes in the NBA.

947 Number of points (947) scored by the Sacramento Kings in the month of April during the 2007-08 season. The Kings best scoring month that year was in March when the team recorded 1,609 points.

948 Number of points (948) scored by Pete Chilcutt during his stay in Sacramento from 1992-94. Chilcutt started 35 games for the Kings during that timeframe and his career points per game average over nine NBA seasons was 4.3.

949 The number of points (949) recorded by Arnie Risen during his 1954 season with the Rochester Royals. That year, Risen averaged 13.2 points per game; second best on the team.

950 Team leading career number of steals (950) by a Kings franchise player, recorded by Sam Lacey from 1970-81. Although the

NBA did not record the number of steals a player earned during Lacey's first three seasons in the league, he still managed to record 999 official thefts.

951 Number of assists (951) tallied by Wayne Embry during his eight seasons with the Cincinnati Royals. Over his career, Embry recorded a total of 1,194 lend-a-hands with Cincinnati, Boston, and Milwaukee.

952 Points per game average (95.2) recorded by Kings' opponents during the 2002-03 season. The Kings averaged 101.7 ppg themselves en route to a 59-23 record.

953 The number of minutes (953) played by Kevin Gamble during his 1997 season with the Sacramento Kings. Gamble completed his career in 1997 with 14,508 minutes played.

954 Number of offensive rebounds (954) secured by Eddie Johnson during his stint with the Kansas City and Sacramento Kings from 1982 through 1987. During his career, Johnson collected over 1,780 offensive boards.

955 Number of points (955) scored by Bob Davies during his 1951 season with the World Champion Rochester Royals. That season, the 6'1" guard/forward popped in 326 field goals and 303 free throws.

956 Number of free throw attempts (956) posted by Doug Christie during his time in Sacramento from 2001 through 2005. During this timeframe, Christie popped in 825 charity shots and averaged 10.6 points per game.

957 Effective field goal percentage (.957) on dunks attempted by Brad Miller during the 2007-08 season. Of Miller's shot attempts, 3% were dunk shots, 3% were tips, 26% were inside the paint, and 68% were jump shots.

958 Points per game average (95.8) tallied by the 1955-56 Rochester Royals. The team completed the season with a 29-43 record and a third place finish in the Western Division.

959 Minutes played (959) during Tariq Abdul-Wahad's rookie season with the Kings during the 1998 NBA campaign. Abdul-Wahad was selected out of San Jose State as the Kings' only first round pick in the 1997 draft. Tariq was born as Olivier Michael Saint-Jean, but changed his name when he converted to Islam in 1997. He is the first player to be born and brought-up in France to grace the NBA hardwood.

960 Number of points (960) scored by Med Park during his stint with the Cincinnati Royals from 1959-60. While in Cincy, Park averaged nine points per game and 2.7 assists per contest.

961 Number of points (961) surrendered by the Cincinnati Royals vs. the New York Knicks during the teams' 1958 meetings. The Royals scored 921 points in the nine games played and ended with a 4-5 record.

962 Field goal attempts (962) by Sacramento's Ron Artest during his 2007-08 season with the Kings. The number 16 pick in the 1999 NBA draft scored 1,168 points in 2008 while draining 436 of his shots.

963 Number of points (963) scored by Nate Williams during the Cincinnati Royals' 1971-72 season. Williams logged 2,173 minutes in 81 games and averaged 11.9 points per game that year.

964 Number of points (964) scored by the Kings' Brad Miller during his 2007-08 season in Sacramento. Miller clocked in 2,513 minutes of playing time and shot 337-728 from the field that year.

965 Number of games (965) played during former Sacramento King Joe Kleine's NBA career that spanned three decades. Kleine retired from basketball in 2000 and finished with 1,902 shots made.

966 Number of points (966) scored by former Cincinnati Royal Tom Van Arsdale during his 1967 season with Detroit, the year before moving over to Cincinnati.

967 Points per game average (96.7) by the Sacramento Kings during the 1991 NBA season. That year, the Kings finished seventh in their division and surrendered 103.5 points per game.

968 Field goal attempts (968) logged by Nate Williams and the number of total rebounds (968) snagged by Sam Lacey during their 1972 season with the Cincinnati Royals.

969 The number of points (969) scored by the 1959 Cincinnati Royals during their nine games with the New York Knicks. The Royals allowed 1,044 points during their nine game series and came away with a 3-6 record.

970 Points per game average (97.0) surrendered by the 2001-02 Sacramento Kings. Fortunately for SAC fans, the Kings averaged 104.6 points per game themselves, leading to a 61-21 finish and a Pacific Division crown.

971 Number of points (971) scored by Sacramento's Francisco Garcia during his 2007-08 season with the Kings. Garcia chipped in 348 field goals on 753 attempts. His 971 points were fourth best on the squad that year.

972 Number of career blocks (972) collected by former KC and Sacramento King LaSalle "Tank" Thompson. The former University of Texas standout wore the jersey number 41 throughout his NBA career with four different teams including the Kings, Pacers, 76ers, and Nuggets.

973 Month and year (9/73) that Nate Archibald signed a seven year contract with the Kansas City Kings for $450,000.

974 Number of points (974) surrendered by the 1973 Kansas City Kings during games played in October. That month, the Kings

scored 904 points of their own and recorded a 3-6 record. Their best month was in November when the Kings posted an 11-4 record.

975 Pace Factor, (97.5) which is the estimated number of possessions by a team per 48 minutes of play, by the 1993-94 Sacramento Kings. That year, the Kings averaged 101.1 points per game.

976 Number of three pointers (976) made by 11 season veteran Walt Williams during his NBA career. In 1993, Williams was named to the second team All-Rookie squad after averaging 17 points a game and swiping 66 steals for the Sacramento Kings. The seventh overall pick in the 1992 draft finished his career with 8,385 points.

977 Month and year (9/77) that the Kings signed 6'8" free agent Bob Nash. He is currently the men's basketball coach at the University of Hawaii.

978 Points per game average (97.8) surrendered by the Kings during the 2004 season. Sacramento outscored their opponent 102.8-97.8 that year, finishing second in the Pacific Division.

979 Year and month (97/9) that the Sacramento Kings signed free agent and three time world champion Stacey King. The next month, Sacramento waived him and King never played for the Kings.

980 Month and year (9/80) that the Kings acquired Jo Jo White from the Golden State Warriors for future cash considerations. Jo Jo White won two NBA titles with the Boston Celtics and was the 1976 NBA Finals MVP. White also won a gold medal at the 1968 Mexico City Olympics.

981 Month and year (9/81) that former Sacramento King Danny Ainge played his final Major League Baseball game for the Toronto Blue Jays. Ainge made his MLB debut on May 21, 1979 and went 3 for 4 with one RBI.

982 Points per game average (98.2) recorded by the 1995 Sacramento Kings. The Kings finished the season in fifth place after their

defense surrendered 99.2 ppg. Fortunately, Mitch Richmond earned his $3 million in salary and delighted SAC fans with 22.8 points per game.

983 Month and year (9/83) that the Kings signed Larry Drew to a five year contract. The former University of Missouri standout finished his NBA career with 8,110 points on 3,308 field goals made.

984 Year and month (98/4) that the Kings closed out their 50th season in franchise history and 13th in the Sacramento area. It was also the fourth consecutive season the Kings recorded a winning record at home.

985 Number of field goal attempts (985) posted by Mike Bibby during his 2001-02 season with the Kings. That year, Bibby dropped in 446 of those shots and averaged 13.7 points per game.

986 Month and year (9/86) that the Kings signed first round draft pick Harold Pressley to a four year contract. Before making the leap to the NBA, Pressley became the first player in Big East history to record a triple double while playing at Villanova.

987 Number of offensive rebounds (987) pulled down by the 2001 Sacramento Kings. Sacramento was led that year by Vlade Divac's 207 offensive boards while Chris Webber led all King glass cleaners with 777 total rebounds.

988 Year and month (98/8) that the Kings opted not to renew the contract of assistant coach Mike Bratz. Bratz played in Sacramento for one season, tallying 70 points.

989 Points per game average (98.9) posted by the 2006 Kings. Sacramento outscored their opponents 98.9 to 97.3 while recording a 44-38 record; good enough for a fourth place finish in the Pacific Division.

990 Points per game average (99.0) surrendered by the Kings versus the Minnesota Timberwolves during the teams' 74 meetings

through the 2008 NBA campaign. Unfortunately for SAC fans, the Wolves hold a 39-35 edge in head-to-head competition.

991 Defensive rating (99.1), which is points allowed per 100 possessions, for the 2002-03 Sacramento Kings. That year, the Kings finished the season with a .720 winning percentage and a 59-23 record.

992 Number of field goal attempts (992) tossed up by Bob Boozer during his 1962-63 season with the Cincinnati Royals. That year, Boozer connected on 440 shots and dropped in 1,132 points; fourth best on the club.

993 Pace Factor (99.3) of the 1999-2000 Sacramento Kings. This was the best Pace Factor in the league as the Kings finished the season with a 44-38 record.

994 Square miles (994) of Sacramento County which covers the city of Sacramento, the state capitol. As of 2006, the population was 1,347,799; mostly King fans.

995 Team leading number of points (995) scored by Arnie Risen during the 1948-49 Rochester Royals season. Risen finished the year with a 16.6 points per game average.

996 Minutes (996) played by Doug Christie during his 2004-05 season with the Kings. That year, Christie found playing time in 31 games and averaged 32.1 minutes played per contest.

997 Year and month (99/7) that the Kings renewed Assistant Coach Pete Carril's contract. That month, the Kings also signed Assistant Coach Byron Scott to a contract extension.

998 Field goal attempts (998) by Walt Williams during his 1995 season with the Sacramento Kings. Although Williams was close, no one other than Mitch Richmond put up over 1,000 shots on the season. Richmond jacked up 1,497 shots that year en route to a 22.8 points per game average.

999 Radio station, KRCX (99.9 FM), in Sacramento that broadcasts all Kings' games in Spanish. Tune in and hear Armando Botello give play-by-play of each Kings game. Also, the month and year (9/99) that the Kings re-signed forward Corliss Williamson. That year, Corliss scored 785 points, grabbed 290 boards, and dished out 82 assists.

1000 The winning percentage (1.000) recorded by the Rochester Royals in games played against the Waterloo Hawks, the Denver Nuggets, and the Anderson Packers during the 1949-50 season. The Nuggets and Hawks had a combined record of 30 wins and 124 losses. Even though the Packers made it to the semifinals that year, none of the three teams would return the following year. The Royals posted 2-0 records against all three teams, and captured six of their 51 wins on the season.

Bibliography

We do extensive research for all of our titles, and because we know fans like us want to have access to as much material as possible we take great pride in making our own website interactive for our readers—but in addition to that, we also want to make sure we provide a helpful list of all the sources that provide us with information as we write.

The National Basketball Association at www.nba.com has done an amazing job of making statistics available to fans. The individual team sites offer detailed franchise histories, and a virtual clearinghouse of player information from past and present. For this Sacramento Kings title, we used www.nba.com/kings.We also used www.espn.com and www.basketball-reference.com extensively, but we verified all statistics through the NBA site, and when discrepancies arose we always defaulted to the numbers put out by the National Basketball Association.

Our preferred method of research is actually to dig through piles and piles of old, dusty copies of *Sports Illustrated*, *Sporting News*, and *Sport* magazines as well as old *Kings Media Guides* programs—and we did that, a lot—but technology being what it is today, we also made good use of LexisNexis to cull through decades of Associated Press Internet articles and visited www.82games.com, www.amazon.com, www.Forbes.com, www.stubhub.com, and also *Yahoo!* Sports. Two other frequently visited sites include www.grandstandsports.com and www.coolstandings.com.

Our personal libraries are filled with books on basketball. *The Official NBA Encyclopedia* (3rd edition), edited by Jan Hubbard, is one of the best. It proved to be a valuable resource. We also used *The Best Book of Basketball Facts and Stats*, by Marty Strasen and *Sporting News – Official NBA Guide 2006-07*.

Of course, any mistakes found in these pages are our own.

Finally, if you do not own a copy of *Reynolds Remembers: 20 Years with the Sacramento Kings* by Jerry Reynolds with Don Drysdale, make sure to get one soon!

Index